Nov. 9, 19__

I can't believe how differ__ things are now from the last ___ntry in here. Tara revealed her disorder, went in the hos__ (all) due to the depre___ ___s will scared all of us, and ___ have been here 1 week. ___ have come to doubt just about everything – especially my parenting. I sitting here in bed reading <u>Through Divided Minds</u> (about MPD) and can't help (not the 1st time) wonder what awful things might have (and statistically do in many cases) caused this in our family. In spite of this I have not yet gone back to self-hatred & some of my more typical reactions of days long ago. That rather surpries me, especially since there is ___ reason to

CH

DISCARD
AUG 2003
WESTMINSTER PUBLIC LIBRARY
3705 W. 112TH AVE.
WESTMINSTER, CO 80031

# THE
# ANOREXIA
# DIARIES

## A MOTHER and DAUGHTER'S TRIUMPH over Teenage Eating Disorders

**LINDA M. RIO
AND TARA M. RIO**
with advice and commentary from
**Craig Johnson, Ph.D.**

RODALE

Notice

The medical information in this book is for reference only. It is designed to help you make informed decisions about your child's behavior and emotional health. It is not intended as a substitute for any treatment that may have been prescribed by your child's doctor or psychologist. If you suspect that your child has a medical or psychological problem, we urge you to seek competent medical help.

Internet addresses and telephone numbers given in this book were accurate at the time it went to press.

© 2003 by Linda M. Rio and Tara M. Rio

All rights reserved. No part of this publication may be reproduced or transmitted in any form or by any means, electronic or mechanical, including photocopying, recording, or any other information storage and retrieval system, without the written permission of the publisher.

Publisher's Note:
Tara's and Linda's diaries have been edited when necessary for relevance, clarity, and space. Other changes from the original diaries, as transcribed by the authors, were made for spelling, correction of dates, and to change the names of individuals for matters of privacy.

Printed in the United States of America
Rodale Inc. makes every effort to use acid-free ∞ , recycled paper ♻ .

Cover photograph © Brad Wilson/Photonica
Interior photograph © Phil Nee
Book design by Tara Long

**Library of Congress Cataloging-in-Publication Data**

Rio, Linda M.
   The anorexia diaries : a mother and daughter's triumph over teenage eating disorders / Linda M. Rio and Tara M. Rio, with advice and commentary from Craig Johnson.
       p.      cm.
   Includes index.
   ISBN 1–57954–729–X hardcover
   1. Rio, Tara M.—Health. 2. Rio, Tara M.—Diaries. 3. Rio, Linda M.—Diaries. 4. Anorexia nervosa—Patients—United States—Diaries. 5. Anorexia nervosa—Patients—United States—Family relationships. 6. Mothers and daughters. I. Rio, Tara M. II. Johnson, Craig, date. III. Title.
   RC552.A5R547 2003
   616.85'262'0092—dc21                                    2003005772

**Distributed to the book trade by St. Martin's Press**

2   4   6   8   10   9   7   5   3   1   hardcover

 **RODALE**
WE **INSPIRE** AND **ENABLE** PEOPLE TO IMPROVE
THEIR LIVES AND THE WORLD AROUND THEM

FOR MORE OF OUR PRODUCTS
**WWW.RODALESTORE**.COM
(800) 848-4735

*For Ashlee, Shyann, and Carli*
*May you learn from the struggles and triumphs*
*of the generations of women who came before you and leave*
*an enduring legacy for the generations of girls to follow.*

# CONTENTS

## FOREWORD

Recently, I was at a board meeting of the National Eating Disorders Association. There were several new members attending, and we were all introducing ourselves and explaining why we were involved with the field. When the introductions came to one of our new female members, a highly accomplished attorney in her fifties, she hesitantly commented, "This is every woman's secret." Although she had never struggled with anorexia or bulimia per se, she revealed that she lived with a persistent self-consciousness and dissatisfaction with her size and shape. Despite her many successes and obvious attractiveness, she harbored a sense of shame about her body that profoundly affected her feelings about herself. In fact, this feeling that she was "fat" or wasn't "measuring up" regarding her size and shape tended to be her predominant feeling about herself, trumping all other positive attributes. Unfortunately, this is a common experience among many American women regardless of their age, appearance, or success in life.

Linda and Tara Rio's diaries offer readers an unusual opportunity to see how this "secret" can explode into an eating disorder. Rarely have I seen such a story told with so much honesty and candor. And unlike the dramatic portrayals of eating disorders seen in movies and television shows, the Rios' story is a real-life, classic account of what can happen to an ordinary American family.

In my work, I'm often asked to recommend a book that will help families who are struggling with eating disorders to better understand and cope with the disease. With the publication of this book, I now have that resource. Linda and Tara's diary entries are excellent examples of how a fear of "fat" can become the concrete representation of millions of women's fear of "not measuring up." And while other books provide isolated glimpses into the lives of people struggling with anorexia or bulimia, they often fail to tell the whole story. With this book, the full spectrum of the disease is revealed for the first time—a spectrum that includes the often profound impact on the rest of the family.

At times, Tara and Linda's story may be painful to read, particularly when it sounds a little too familiar to your own family's story. Though each of our circumstances is different, we *all* grapple with the same insecurities, fears, and miscommunication problems that the Rios experienced. Yet, in the end, their story is one of hope and inspiration. It is the story of a family that, when pushed to the point of crisis, learned to pull together instead of pulling apart.

—*Craig Johnson, Ph.D.*
*Director, Eating Disorders Program*
*Laureate Psychiatric Clinic and Hospital*
*Tulsa, Oklahoma*

# INTRODUCTION

It seems like I've been writing in a diary for as long as I can remember. Keeping diaries has been a family tradition, something my mother passed along to me as I have to my daughters. Held sacred to the women in our family, diaries served as a secret outlet to divulge our innermost thoughts and emotions.

As a young girl, I would begin each new diary promising to write every day. Inevitably, a month later I would stuff it in my nightstand drawer, quickly losing interest. But I would always pick it up again at times when I was upset and needed an outlet to express my frustration, anger, and sadness. I think I really began to depend on my diary as a source of comfort when I was about 8.

I was always aware that my mother kept a diary as well. I would go in to say goodnight to her and see her lying in bed feverishly writing about the day's events. What I didn't know was that she also began using a diary at a young age. I think I was about 12 when my mom let me read her diary from her preteen and teen years. This gesture meant the world to me. The idea that she trusted me with her most intimate thoughts both shocked and delighted me. Reading through my mother's adolescent feelings made me realize that she actually had been a teenager at one time, an idea entirely foreign to me up until then. I instantly gained a new kind of respect and understanding for her. A resilient bond developed that would later prove helpful to us as we navigated through troubled waters.

The next time my mom let me read her diaries was a couple of years ago. She was cleaning out some of her things when she came across the entries she had written during my illness. As I began to read her desperate, pain-filled words, an overwhelming sense of empathy came over me, along with inescapable feelings of guilt and sadness. As we sat together on the floor of her bedroom with damp eyes, one phrase kept coming out of my mouth, "I had no idea you felt that way."

That night I went home and pulled out some of my old diaries from the same time period. As I apprehensively read my teenage entries, I was stunned to see how, regardless of our good intentions, my mom and I perceived things in drastically different ways. It seemed as if the two of us weren't even living in the same house during my teen years. It was frustrating to realize we had the same goals but couldn't connect with each other enough to achieve them. It was out of this frustration that the book you now hold in your hands was born.

I believe our experiences are common among mothers and daughters. We hope that in hearing our story and reading snapshots of our thoughts and feelings from that arduous time, other mothers and daughters will be able to find the connection that took us so long to discover. By examining both sides of the teen-parent divide, we hope this book gives readers a greater sense of empathy and tolerance for each other to help reduce the gap of misunderstandings within families.

*Sara Rio*

Diaries have always played an important role in my life. I started keeping my first diary when I was 12 years old. My older half-brother, whom I met only a couple of times, sent it to me in the mail. I cherished this very small, white, vinyl-covered book. It had a small lock with a key, and, most important, gold edges on the pages. I loved to run my fingers over those shiny, smooth edges.

It has never been easy to go back and read my diaries, and it was especially difficult delving into pages and pages of my hand-written diary accounts of the years that my daughter, Tara, suffered from eating disorders. But I knew I had to. As a mother, I had to know if my diaries revealed any clues as to why my daughter struggled so much during her adolescence. As I spent hours poring over my old diary pages, it sometimes felt as if I were picking through the sand and rock of an archeological site, unearthing the history of our family's ups and downs.

Once I began reading, I discovered a lot—maybe too much at times yet not enough to completely understand Tara's situation. Not until years later, when Tara approached me with the idea of putting this book together, and not until I had the incredible experience of reading my daughter's thoughts written in her own hand as she went through this terrible time, did I fully appreciate the depth of her pain and the miracle of our triumph. It's not easy to lay bare the secrets of our family. We're not perfect. We're not heroes or even role models. But we're a family that stayed together during a difficult time. We've shared our story, warts and all, in the hope that in some way it will help your family to understand each other better. With this understanding, we know you, too, can triumph over the challenges in your lives.

*Linda M. Rio*

## TARA'S DIARY

### 8/25/89

Last night I asked my mom some questions about bulimia and anorexia, like what throwing up did to your teeth and what problems it could cause your body. I thought that for sure she would know what I was doing to myself.

How could a mother not know the terrible things her daughter was doing?

## LINDA'S DIARY

### August 25, 1989

Tara approached me last night. She asked me a lot of weird questions. She scares me. I hope I answered her questions. I like it when she talks to me, but I don't know sometimes if she just wants to talk about just anything or whether it means something more. She hates me so much right now for not being here for her all the time. I can't seem to be able to reach her. I am working a lot this week and don't get to see her much during the week...

PART I

# THE
# DIARIES

## CHAPTER 1, 1973–1985
## OUR PERFECT FAMILY
### *"I hate to keep writing depressing things, but . . ."*

In this book, you'll read the personal thoughts my mother and I recorded in our diaries beginning in the years before I developed an eating disorder and continuing through my years of treatment and therapy. In order to understand our thoughts and feelings, you'll need to know a bit about our family. My mom grew up in Carlsbad, California, just north of San Diego, during the 1950s and 1960s. She was the only child of her German-Scotch-Irish parents. Though her family was financially comfortable, my mother's life was anything but. After years of fighting, drinking, and infidelities, her parents separated when she was 14. My mother spent her formative years at an all-girl Catholic high school, her only comfort coming from the other girls in her class and from the nuns.

My dad grew up in New Britain, Connecticut, the only son of his Italian, working-class parents. He and his two sisters love to share stories of their mischievous young adventures, and my grandmother loves to tell stories of her subsequent harsh punishments. Living as typical Italians, their household was always filled with yelling, unnecessary drama, and, of course, food. Seeking an escape from this anxiety-producing environment, my dad quit high school to join the Navy and left home at the age of 17.

Dad's Navy adventures led him to San Diego, where he ended up living next door to my mother while she attended her first semester of college. After dating only a couple of months, my mom got pregnant at the age of 18. They married almost immediately, and 9 months later, in 1969, my brother, Gregg, was born.

Now that he had a family to support, my dad embarked on his 34-year career with Xerox. Struggling to define her role as a young mother amidst the dramatic political changes of the early 1970s, my mom longed for what she had given up—college, a career, and independence. I came along in 1973 after my mother, watching my brother play in the sand at the beach by himself, decided he looked lonely and needed the company of a sibling.

My early memories are of a very happy family. My mom would walk me to school each day, quizzing me on my spelling words as we traveled down the dirt road with our dogs in tow. My dad would often come home from work hiding M&M's behind his back—peanut for my brother and plain for me. He'd throw them to us from across the room and let us eat them immediately, whether or not we had already eaten dinner. A medley of chickens, cats, pigs, and a pony rounded out our family unit.

Like most families, though, ours was not without its problems. And I remember those as well.

My father is a workaholic, type A personality. He was brought up to believe in the value of hard work and providing for your family—all great ideals. However, this strong work ethic kept him away from home often. When he wasn't traveling on business trips, he would leave for work around 5:30 A.M. and return home around 8:30 P.M. He was full of life and energy. But that energy could be channeled into a fun, exciting, and spontaneous man or an angry, impatient, and critical one. We never really knew which man would arrive home from work. One day it was a carefree, enthusiastic father, another day he would be yelling at someone before he even walked in the door. My father was under a lot of stress and wasn't able to hide it. As a child, I wasn't able to understand the extreme amount of pressure he experienced. I didn't appreciate all the hard work and dedication he showed toward providing for his family. I saw only the frustrations he struggled with. He was loud and angry, and it scared me. I remember almost holding my breath when I would hear his car enter the garage, hoping it was going to be a good day. If it was a bad day, Mom and Dad would fight all through dinner, and Dad would end up throwing something across the dinner table and sending us to our rooms. Yet despite the fear I felt around him at times, I also adored him. He was my hero. I admired his wisdom and strength, and I searched for ways to please him.

As a child, I spent a lot of time outdoors playing pretend. One day, I was a loving young mommy wrapping my cats up in baby blankets and pushing them around in a stroller in the front yard. The next day, I was a fashion model striking a pose on our backyard deck while my apathetic brother reluctantly snapped pictures of me. I created a pretend world that inoculated me from the reality of our family's struggles.

It warms my heart to read about how much my mom seemed to love me and cherish me in these early years. And it doesn't surprise me. I remember feeling loved and cherished, especially by her. I felt incredibly bonded to her. But as I got older, she seemed to pull away and feel smothered by me. In turn I felt rejected and abandoned.

My brother and I were not close as kids. As my dad used to say, shit rolls down hill. My dad yelled at my mom, my mom yelled at Gregg, and Gregg yelled at me. I felt like he resented me for not being "disciplined" as much as he was. He was the male in the family, and my dad had different expectations for him. He bore the brunt of my dad's violent outbursts, just as my dad had borne the brunt of his father's. I wanted desperately to be accepted by my older brother, following him around and playing with Star Wars miniatures just because he liked them. There were rare occasions, usually when my mom had sent us both to our rooms, that we united together against her. These were the times we laughed uncontrollably as my mom screamed at us from the other room. And, of course, the more we upset her, the funnier it was.

I didn't understand my mom's need to work outside the home. I remember, as a toddler, feeling lost when she left me at the church day care. Tears streaming down my face, I would watch her get in her car and drive away. I understood her desire to go back to school even less. To me it seemed that once she started school she turned into this stressed-out woman who never got a moment's peace—which is probably pretty accurate. She was constantly reading textbooks and writing papers. And she was the queen of multitasking. It seemed rare that I ever had her undivided attention. I interpreted that to mean I wasn't worthy of her full attention.

On the other hand, when I was in grade school, I remember feeling so proud of my mom. On the rare occasion that she would come to school, all my friends would comment on how pretty she was. And when they asked me what she did, I was proud to say that she was a therapist who helped people. Most of my friends' moms just stayed at home. My mom was a walking saint—keeping a house, raising two kids, and counseling the world.

My parents' fighting scared me. And during the times they were arguing, it would be like walking on eggshells. One wrong move, and the angry outbursts would be turned against us kids. I grew up with the instability of believing my family was going to get torn apart at any minute. But I also believed that my mom and dad's interactions were normal. I didn't have another frame of reference to compare it to. I thought all my friends' parents would be loudly fighting one minute and making out in the kitchen the next. It wasn't until I went to college and got some distance from home that I objectively saw the roller coaster of their married life.

Though I felt abandoned by my mom, I don't think those feelings were solely associated with her spending so much time on her career. I was angry with her for not protecting my brother and me from my dad's angry outbursts. She didn't stick up for us and defend our basic safety needs. Being angry with my dad was too scary; therefore, my mom received the brunt of my rage.

The entries you are about to read are from my mother's diary. They begin in the fall of 1978, when she was just 28 and I was starting kindergarten. At the time, we had just moved into my parents' dream house—a custom-built ranch home on an acre of land in the outskirts of San Diego.

## LINDA'S DIARY

*September 11, 1978*
Tara's First Day of Kindergarten

**First Day**
*For my mother then*
*for my daughter now*
*I left my little girl today.*
*The memory will remain.*
*As my mother left me it is*
*for her joy, once mine; now pain.*
*I left her smiling, happy, free*
*As I've been told she left me when*

*I too went forth to life, my own.*
*A child's footsteps pass where a baby's have been.*
*I left her to strangers, this*
*is my baby, my child!*
*But I had no fear, as I remember now;*
*I must have looked up too, as she, and just smiled.*
*I left her to herself,*
*to begin to be,*
*to grow, to learn. That today*
*she is more a part of her, and less a part of me.*
*I left her.*
*As I must*
*sustain the cycle, continue the plan.*
*To herself, to god, to the world I entrust.*

*September 12, 1978*

Second Day of School

It still hurts.

I came home yesterday and wrote a poem about Tara leaving for school. I only walked her to the gate today (yesterday walked her to her class). She wore her gauchos (pants) and pink top, white sweater cape. She walked with Casey, Maya, and Lanie. Gregg was ahead with Mike and Jeff. I told him to be sure she got to her classroom, but even if he didn't I knew she'd be all right and find it. She walked about halfway across the field laughing and talking with friends. She walked with me watching. Then, when I figured she had forgotten all about me, she turned and yelled, "Bye, Momma." Gregg did too after.

Yes it still hurts to know those cherished years are gone for both my children. They will have their own lives, worlds to live, and so must I. It's funny, though, for so long I've been involved in so much—Red Cross, backyard swim, working, taking classes—that "my time" seemed to conflict or be inhibited by the children's time. Now, I'm not into much of anything and I want to hold on to them and they are letting go.

*Tuesday, September 26, 1978*

I find myself just staring at Tara lately. She's so cute coming across the school yard. She cried so much yesterday when her lunch sack split open and applesauce got on everything. Sometimes she's so big to me, and others—still a baby.

*Friday, September 29, 1978*

Heard late last night that Pope John Paul I died, only a pope for one month. Disasters and deaths of late are hitting me, bombarding me. I feel like it is too much—that some omnipotent power is trying to tell us something.

Louie has been gone since Wednesday—just to San Marcos—I was very lonely—haven't gone anywhere. I don't leave the house much anymore—no money anyhow. Still (after 28½ years) trying to decide what to do—work full-time (fighting that thought), part-time (if I can afford it), go back to school (money and time and trouble), or just stay here for one more year and finish on volunteering and working with the kids.

*Friday, November 3, 1978*

I've been feeling so crummy—about me, my life. I flunked the typing test yesterday. I really thought I could do it if I had to. I cried in the shower last night, today too (not in the shower). I don't want to talk to Louie, but I probably will—he's heard all this stuff before. He was teasing me last night about not being able to do anything, being selfish and self-centered. It wasn't funny to me because that's how I feel.

I looked at the women yesterday taking the test and all I could think about was losers. One was talking about her divorce—she had to leave because she couldn't type at all. I'm scared that if I had to, I couldn't get a job—and if I could, what would it be—nothing.

Oh, I get like this whenever I'm inactive for a while, sooner or later I'll get over it.

I'm just such a dunce. I wait for someone to show me the way— open up my life—that's not going to happen.

I tried to clean the house good today (If I can't make money, at least do something here)—I put a huge hole in the kitchen vinyl floor doing it!

I have a terrible desire to be someone special, even if it's in a very small realm. I figure that what I have is a bad case of an inferiority complex.

*Sunday, March 3, 1979*

As usual, been meaning to write. Tara is reading. She has been for about 3 to 4 weeks now. I got a Janet and Mark book they were giving away at school. After going through it just once, she just started reading it. She is very eager to learn and study. I really am amazed by her sometimes, and try not to act like a doting parent, but think she has real capabilities. Of course, she could just be eager in her young age. I must try not to squelch it though, and work with her over the summer.

We talked about me going to school. My mom came over Wednesday and left Friday to watch Gregg and Tara while I taught CPR at school for Professional Growth Day. Gregg started Little League practice Friday and pitched the last inning, not bad either, but he thought he was the greatest!

*Saturday, March 31, 1979*

I've been thinking more and more about going back to school. There is a mixture of fear, cheapness, laziness, and a whole lot of lack of decision about it. I probably won't have a job with the school district, so it would be a time to start, and Louie said I could (money-wise, although I don't know where it would come from). Gas shortages are predicted, besides I really don't want to work full-time with career stuff for several years (if I can help it). I would like to try to help the kids with their school work as much as possible—and I don't do as much of that now as I'd like.

## July 1, 1979

Louie and I started off with an argument—luckily he was smart enough to see it as a result of built-up tensions.

Had a party for Tara's birthday—Mary, Maya, Terri, Judy, and Rhonda came. 1:00-3:00. We had a cake and ice cream, played games. Tara cried, and got selfish and nasty. I hate what Christmas and birthdays do to kids.

We went to see the movie Superman tonight. Tara is tired, had Kristin sleep over last night. You're a sweetheart, baby.

## September 15, 1979

Last night we registered me for National University. We then met friends for dinner for their anniversary.

[Author's Note: I enrolled in college to complete my bachelor's degree, with a major in behavioral science.]

## September 28, 1979

Tara looked so small yesterday after my being around high school kids all day. She's been bringing surprises home in her lunch box, pictures with "I love you mom," and a penny.

[Author's Note: I began working part-time at a local high school in late September.]

*Halloween, October 31, 1979*

Another holiday come and gone and I yearn even more with each passing one for the years of my children's lives that have already passed so quickly. My feet ache from walking up and down hills, in and out of streets. I was starved when we came home to quickly eat dinner then gobbled as many candy bars as I could (my twice a year treat now and Easter). I was cold (with a cold and cough)—but still know how much I will miss this in such a short time when Gregg and Tara will be too old for this. Tara ran to every house tonight—Gregg wanted us to stay away from him and Mike—but later didn't seem to mind too much.

I popped into the shower—and when came out heard Tara snoring in our bed. She never said good-night, just collapsed. She's such an angel. Gregg would try to go on forever.

Louie and I are on bad terms since Sunday—an argument—drains us both, but he is carrying such a heavy load with work and school—such a heavy pace.

[Author's Note: Lou attended undergraduate classes at National University in San Diego.]

*December 26, 1979*

I have had little time for much lately, most of all reflective writing. Today there is no pressure. I stayed in bed until 8:15 am, then laid down an hour later, just to rest and think.

Louie's parents arrived December 5 and will leave this Friday. Louie was gone a week and a half—in Rochester and then

Connecticut. He left right after Thanksgiving weekend and got home one day before his parents. That one day was very important to us. He put his ring back on then . . .

[Author's Note: After one of our very serious arguments, Louie actually removed his wedding ring for a few days. We talked seriously about separating or divorcing, but in the end, did not.]


*February 1, 1980 (Day before my 30th birthday)*

Last day of my twenties.

I have told myself for months that this would be no big deal. But right now I'd like to crawl into a hole and stay there, at least until tomorrow is over. Louie wanted to have a party—a sweet thought—but he hasn't been around to help with anything. I usually like to be in the limelight, but not now. I just wish I could go away.

It's not that 30 is so old. It is a different decade. Twenty is still young, youthful, not on the downward side. I know that from here on in, age will come, the wrinkles and gray hair and flab will appear, not all of a sudden, but the shortness of life is suddenly very apparent to me. Also, it is so damn shitty how the body ages, but inside, in my mind and heart I feel 18.


*February 12, 1980*

Louie is under terrible pressures. We haven't spoken since Sat. when I issued a complaint—he reacted (I think over) and so I left him alone to get over it. Well, I found out last night that the reason why he got (or stayed) angry is because I wasn't talking to him, so he felt unloved. I think he is letting everything bother him . . . I hate his company so many times lately. I hate the rat race of the world, and the pain involved. I wish we could go somewhere and make a modest living and enjoy life. Louie is not yet ready for that though. I sometimes wonder if he'll live long enough to ever enjoy life.

*April 7, 1980*

Easter was yesterday. We went to mass. Tara wore the new pink gingham outfit I got for her. Church was crowded, but it was nice to see that people still got dressed up in pretty pastels and observed Easter. On Good Friday we all went to Balboa Park to roller skate and go to the museum of man and the space theater. Saturday was spent on yard work (in back), getting Easter bunnies for Gregg and Tara, and me baking. My mom and Granny came over for dinner. The kids got up at 5:30 am. (I'd gotten up at 4:30 am to put the rabbits out and hide more eggs). They were thrilled with the bunnies. Louie and I had stayed up until 12:30 am hiding eggs and making baskets. We were tired, but the kids kept on going. Before all this, last week, Louie and I seriously considered breaking up, again.

The weird part was that we never had an argument to provoke it. It was all done calmly, realizing that we both love each other. There are some basic problems that we've always had, and the newer one of our lives separating.

*April 16, 1980*

I hate to keep writing depressing things, but this crisis with Louie and me is certainly not over and it's more than a three-day silent treatment. We talked again last night. We're not angry or anything, just not sure of where we stand. It all seems so temporary, like standing on unsure ground. We decided that we might be reflecting a pattern, or trend of forces outside ourselves. We figured we could try and see if it will end. I thought we'd need to be very much aware of what is happening, and have to try very hard just to maintain. There are so many things that make it so difficult, and yet inside we still have those feelings that we should be able to "make it" forever.

*July 4, 1980*

Tara's birthday was Tuesday. My mom and Aunt Lois came over Monday to give her lots (as usual) of presents—garage sale kitchen and all accessories. That wore me out. Tues. she had 4 friends over for a party, they played games, ate pizza, and went in the spa. Of course Gregg caused problems (he said he wouldn't) and of course Tara ended up pouting. There is so much build-up to birthdays. Both kids fell asleep that afternoon.

I had lots to do all week—got little done. Still have to write a paper for my last class. I got real bitchy too—got nervous with the kids' fighting and complaining. The house is bothering me too—walls need to be painted. I feel like I need to demand more for the house, but I'm just too damn cheap—so Louie spends money on what he wants.

*August 1, 1980*

Divorce discussion #434—the one we said we wouldn't have again. Well, jerk that I am brought it up instead of bringing up the problem. I still think it would be easier just to do it and get it over. I still think Louie will leave in a few years. He says he's been wasting his time with me, but I finally today realized and decided that's not my problem or responsibility. If he is unhappy that's his business, not my fault he doesn't do something about it. I have always felt I should leave for his good. No more.

*September 29, 1980*

I have been busy (as shown by my lack of writing in here). There have been a few times this month when I didn't think I could do it all. I've been getting up at 5:30 AM and going constantly until about 11:00 PM—getting to sleep at 11:30 or 12:00. Last week I had a final exam (we didn't know until Wed. night). It was due Sat. morning—5-8 pages. I was up 'til 12:00 AM on Thursday and 1:00 AM Fri.

*Monday, November 24, 1980*

Can't believe I've got a second to write. Louie and I have been talking divorce, again—tried to figure out how we could do it financially. We still love each other—we just argue too much and have so little time together and mutual interests. We spend one moment talking about custody, the other planting new plants around the spa and planning Christmas parties.

Gregg had 3 goals last week in soccer. He really looked good.

*June 1, 1981*

May 31, 1981 Last class—B.A. degree

I think this has got to be the longest void in writing in many, many years. Rather than trying to make up for lost time I will just describe the events of the last couple days.

I spent my last week of school working endlessly on a paper. Louie was in Laguna, Gregg at 6th grade camp. Saturday was my last class, but not graduation day (formally) so I did not expect any surprises at all. I was just thrilled to be done. Louie and the kids had the dining room decorated in yellow and orange streamers. Red roses were on the table with a lovely wonderful note, a chocolate graduation card, Tara made me a card, a graduation cup, and yummy creme and banana cake too! I was " blown away"!

*June 24, 1981*

I cleaned the kids' rooms yesterday—a big job—but other things are undone. I've been home almost two weeks and am still amazed at what is undone around here and how dirty things are—and I'm no clean freak. I verge on boredom sometimes and yet shy away from calling it that because Louie said I would get bored and give everyone a hard time because of it. I so longed for and planned for a time without schedules, time not planned. I hesitate to complain.

I still feel like there is something inside me I need to recover, the peace and serenity. It is like there is a part of me missing. I don't know. I don't think that time alone will cure this. I feel like there is something I have to do (but not accomplish) for myself. Part of it I think has to do with being here, in my home, with the kids. I need to recapture the feeling that this is where I belong.

*Friday, July 31, 1981*

Last week was very busy and hectic. This week, with Louie gone, it was almost too peaceful and calm. I keep waiting for a revelation about my life—the "big light"—perhaps I am just slowly and naturally with the passing of time becoming more and more ready to join the world again. This is a bit of a paradise this summer, to be totally self-controlled, self-limiting. I told myself I would not feel guilty because Louie and most of the rest of the world could not be here too. Except for passing moments, I have kept that one promise.

Last week my mom took the kids and me by train to Los Angeles to see the play "Annie." Tara has been singing (out of key) the songs ever since. Tara has a dance recital coming up. There have been practices and make-up. All bring back vague memories of my dancing days. When I see her with her dancing class, I want to move my feet too and to correct her on certain steps. It makes me want to dance. I wish I had continued lessons, but I rebelled too violently to whatever my mother wanted. Adolescence is such a cheat.

I have been eating a lot (or so it seems)—and many of the "bad" things. I actually feel compelled to eat sweet things—but only at certain times and in high concentrations (candy, cake, ice cream, doughnuts). I even tried to find some info on diabetes or hypoglycemia.

### August 15, 1981

Tara passed advanced beginner swimming level yesterday. She really had a hard time with the elementary backstroke. She kept sinking. She tried not to smile after she got her card, but it was all over her face. Oh, she had her first dance recital last week. I wasn't pleased with the teacher or the level of performance, but the experience was good—the lighting, costumes, technical stuff. It was fun for me to do something with Tara that I had done in the past.

The kids and I have gotten along pretty well all summer, except for the last few days. Gregg and Tara have been fighting. He picks at her and she screams. I usually try to ignore it, but it does finally get to me. Tara says, "You're no kind of a mother!" She says this because I do not come to her rescue. Fun times as a Mother!

*Sunday, September 19, 1981*

I started graduate school this week. When I first went back to school, I was excited and could hardly wait to tell everyone about my classes. Even after a summer's break, I just don't feel that excitement now. Dr. Framo is teaching my 1st course. He had all 70 of us in the lecture hall introduce ourselves and tell about our backgrounds. Half of the students were in the Ph.D. program— almost everyone had such a list of impressive credentials that they could easily be teaching the class! I made my little "speech" as short as possible. I feel so underachieved, unknowledgeable, unable to do all of this! In one moment I am astounded that I am actually a graduate student, wow!—then I feel like I'm in kindergarten starting all over! I don't know how I'll ever have the time (or effort) to do everything.

I came home Thursday night and asked Louie if he just would want to move to Northern CA and open up a little store—a peaceful, no hassle life! He just went back to work after two weeks off—said he almost quit Wed. He's working 14 hr. days and doing terrible.

*Thursday, January 21, 1982*

Tara has been home all week from school. She's had a headache and stomachache. We are starting to get on each other's nerves. She wants attention and love and I'm trying to get schoolwork done. I should have gone to the library several times but haven't gone at all (if I was disciplined enough I would have gone at night) . . .

Louie and I had a good talk on the phone yesterday about tension and stress and how both of us are in the same situation and that we both bring it on ourselves. We talk a lot about whether we could really leave it all and have low-stress jobs—maybe a small store or something. The grass always looks greener.

*September 15, 1983*

Well, the kids are back at school. I must admit my eyes teared up as Gregg went off for his first day at high school. I told him it reminded me of his 1st day at kindergarten. Unfortunately his day was less than ideal—new student, no schedule, no locker, had to ride the city bus home and then ride his bike to soccer because I was working. I so much wanted things to go better for him, but he seems determined and ambitious now.

Tara was enthusiastic as ever and luckily things went better for her. I hate with a passion this uncertainty about the kids' transportation—at times I've felt like I should quit everything and be a full-time chauffeur just so I feel confident about where they are.

*November 1, 1983*

Louie and I fought Halloween night. I packed up and left the room—we missed a Halloween party. The quarter is closing down—don't know how I'll finish—Louie and family are really sick of this. He says I have only one dimension and am boring—he's right.

*June 19, 1985*

Tara had her "celebration" ceremony—leaving 6th grade, on to junior high. It was very nice, with a slide show presentation of the kids doing a take-off of West Side Story. Tara and several others gave speeches before the whole audience. She did really well—Louie was surprised. She looked so cute too in her black and white outfit. We gave her the outfit she just had to have to wear to Magic Mountain (today) and 3 pairs of earrings with a certificate to get her ears double pierced.

Somehow I feel a little sad today. My little girl is growing up (another step) . . .

## LOOKING BACK

## LINDA

I was growing as much as my daughter during these years. I guess we all were. My going back to college put a strain on the whole family. Louie was a very traditional kind of guy. This was pushing those bounds of his image of traditional home life and what family was "supposed to be." His anger scared me, and he seemed to get angry about everything.

I found out about the limits of his anger. On two separate occasions, Lou hit me. This is by far my deepest secret, so deep I didn't write about it in my diary. It is still hard to admit to being hit. At the time, I told only one very, very close friend, and I have told no one since, other than therapists. I felt guilty and wrong. I asked myself many times how could I, a fairly intelligent woman, allow this to happen? I tried hard to be a modern woman of the 1970s, yet found myself making excuses I never would accept from someone else: It was only two times . . . no bones were broken, just bruises. I knew he didn't mean to hurt me; he felt terrible, and I knew he reacted on impulse versus intentional harm. Harm was done, though—more to our relationship than to my body. I found myself thinking thoughts I had heard my clients saying. I played the role of a victim. I didn't speak up and tell him about my own truth; he got to a breaking point. Even this was not enough to face our own ills, as it took our child becoming ill to make us see ourselves, our relationship, more clearly. In the many years since, Lou has apologized and I am no longer fearful, but it is an ugly part of our past.

Why did I "suffer in silence"? I don't really know. I was influenced by a lot of things many other women my age were taught. I was a good Catholic girl. The church taught me to be quiet, stay with my man, and endure pain for the good of strengthening my soul. On the other hand, I was the one who ran for the door when we would argue. My own parents were divorced at a time when divorce was unusual, especially in a Catholic family.

The scars of their divorce were deeply imprinted on my psyche. When I was a teenager, my mother told me to lie to my friends about my dad leaving. During my adolescence I kept my distance from my peers out of fear that they would find out about my family, and that would be too shameful to bear.

My own relationship with my father is complicated. Though I

have a few fond memories of him, I can't say that I ever really knew him. He was quiet, distant, and secretive. I have no wise words or wisdom from him because he rarely talked to my mom and me. He drank too much and stayed away from home a lot. As a young girl, I retrieved him from the bars on many occasions. I saw no affection between my parents. I spent many years expressing vile hatred toward my father. Hate became apathy. Apathy became sadness and loss. Finally, I just came to accept that I would never get what I wanted and stopped trying.

Since I had no emotional connection with my father, I hungered deeply for this with my husband. I admired Louie's passionate devotion to both his children and me. In Louie, I found the qualities I desired most from my own father. The problem was, these wonderful qualities also came with some harsh negatives.

I knew my tumultuous relationship with my husband was not good for my children, so I tried to shield them as much as I knew how at the time. I was very concerned about giving them what I thought I couldn't have—things like self-esteem, freedom, and confidence. Yet despite this, my children—especially Gregg—experienced violence in our home. Louie emotionally abused Gregg, yelling at him and calling him names. There were also many slaps, though no beatings—except to his soul. Tara was slapped as well, but less than her brother. Witnessing the tirades on her brother may have been worse for her. Louie would yell at me for not disciplining the kids enough, for being too soft on them. Since I had no real model of fatherhood from my own dad, I was clueless about what role a father should take. I needed to be stronger as a disciplinarian but purposely tried to compensate for his harshness. I didn't know how to stand up to him, stand up for the kids, or myself. I would often get in the middle between Louie and Gregg. I would just stand there to keep him from hitting Gregg or getting more out of control.

Louie would also be extremely kind and demonstrative in his affection with both the children and me. One minute he would be yelling violently, the next he would want to joke and have fun. I was confused. Louie's ability to be passionately affectionate both physically and verbally was, I think, the salve for all of us. It was hard to stay angry with someone who could also be so kind. He might have been angry, but he was even more intensely sensitive.

I was concerned that in this environment Tara wouldn't be able to grow up to become a strong, independent woman; after all, I certainly didn't feel that way. I tried to be honest with her, which is why I told both my kids about the hitting incidences since they were not present either time. I knew Tara wanted me to change things, but I was helpless to know how. I just kept inching my way along, hoping to find answers. I was hoping schooling would help. It did, a little, eventually, as well as just plain growing up.

It is important for me to stress that we had many, many wonderful times as a family and as a couple, during these years, too. Most of the diary accounts chosen for this book do not reflect the good times. We could not have survived if there had only been negative. We had wonderful holiday times, and we have always celebrated family events with fervor. We went camping, boating, and skiing. We raised dogs, cats, bunnies, chickens, and even pigs at one time, and Tara had a pony. We went to church and did many home projects. We were normal folks.

Unfortunately, as is normal for many women, I think some of my self-doubt was based on my insecurities about my appearance. While I never developed a full-blown eating disorder, I have al-

ways had some distorted thoughts and behaviors about eating.
Even as a skinny teenager, I would diet occasionally. The diets
never lasted, but I somehow thought I was supposed to diet because that's what I read in the teen magazines. I didn't truly believe
I was fat, but I wasn't what I was "supposed" to be. I wanted to
fit in socially but knew I didn't. I read the magazines and compared myself to the models. I read about hair and makeup. I came
up short on everything. As an adult, I verbally put myself down on
a chronic basis. I think part of that was learned through my reli-
gious education. I was taught that one of the worst sins is pride,
and I took that to mean I shouldn't feel good about myself. Sadly,
my daughter watched me through all of this.

Another insecurity that plagued me during these early years was
worry about our finances. I was so busy being fearful about
money that I couldn't truly connect with Tara when she needed me
the most. My worry about the future kept me from being in the
present much of the time.

I felt such pressure to fulfill my mother's dreams for me. She
didn't accomplish what she wanted in life for herself, but she always said that I had so much potential and was so smart. I felt like
a failure—to her and myself—when I chose to have children,
marry, and not attend college. I was so depressed in my own later
teen years that I didn't think I could do anything with my life. I
didn't apply to a 4-year college because I truly did not think I was
smart enough. I started one semester of junior college, but then
dropped out when I found out I was pregnant. I suffered from depression during much of my teen and early years of marriage and
child rearing but never got professional help then. I was the most
deeply depressed, even suicidal, when pregnant with Tara in 1973.
I have never come so close to suicide as one day when sitting alone

in a back bedroom. I was about 5 months pregnant with Tara. My feelings of responsibility for 3½-year-old Gregg were all that kept me alive at that time. I felt totally hopeless, a true failure. I thought I would never attend college or accomplish anything. Two years later, I was a college freshman with two children, totally unsure of where I was going, but at least I was going somewhere. Still, I hadn't completely resolved those feelings, and they resurfaced in my hopes and dreams for Tara as she began adolescence. I unconsciously did exactly what my own mother had done by unwittingly pressuring Tara to succeed.

## CHAPTER 2, 1986–1988
## THE EARLY TEEN YEARS
## *"I HATE THE WAY I LOOK!"*

During the time I wrote the following diary entries, my family felt disjointed. My mom, my dad, my brother, and I were all living separate lives. I would get up in the morning and get dressed, quickly wolf down breakfast, and head off to school. After school I would return home to an empty house. I'd drop off my stuff, grab a snack, and then head down the street to my best friend's house. Her house was full of life and family, and I loved to be there. And when we needed our teenage space we would walk back up the street to my house, knowing no one would ever bother us there. I usually ate dinner with my friend's family or headed home to eat by myself. I would spend the night doing my homework, writing in my diary, and watching TV.

My brother, who was nearly an adult by this time, was rarely home. When he was there, he wanted nothing to do with me. Later, when he left home for college, I remember feeling betrayed by him for leaving me alone in our empty family environment.

My dad would get home around 8:30, and I would reheat his dinner for him and stand in the kitchen while he ate. He would quickly try to take inventory of my day. I would then say goodnight around 9. I would lay in bed awake for at least an hour. I would hear mom walk in the door around 9:30 and would pretend to be asleep when she stopped at my room on the way down the hall. By this time I was so angry with her I couldn't stand to even look at her. And that anger would still be there when I woke up in the morning, ruining the next day. It was a vicious cycle of unresolved hurt.

I don't remember being concerned about being fat until I began puberty and my body began to change. I had always been a thin, active child, so weight was never an issue. But at about the age of 12, fat began to grow on my body in places it never had before. I think physically I was growing into a young woman, but mentally I was still a little girl. The convergence of the two left me confused, frustrated, and uncomfortable. It took another 4 years before the physical symptoms of my eating disorder emerged, but the emotional seeds were being planted throughout my preteen years.

Clearly, my eating habits during these early years were not healthy. And neither was my self-image. I constantly equated the way I looked with how much I ate. And I viewed eating as a weakness, instead of a normal part of human existence. Everything was "black and white" for me. It was good or bad, fat or thin, binge or starve. There was never an in between, no shades of gray.

Likewise, I was experiencing extreme highs and lows in school, particularly when it came to the social aspects of school life. When I began fifth grade, I was one of the most popular girls in school. However, a few weeks after school started, I got into an argument with my best friend. She then, unfortunately, became friends with the school bully. The two of them began to relentlessly torment me every day. They called me names in class, made up evil rumors, and pushed me around when I walked home from school. I went from being the most popular girl in school to the least popular in a matter of days. This torture lasted throughout the school year.

This was about the time my self-esteem took a nosedive. Somewhere about midway through the year, I remember sitting in my bedroom alone after school and taking a fork and pushing the prongs into the skin on the undersides of my wrists. I wondered if I pushed hard enough, if it would puncture a vein. When my mom got home from work I begged her to transfer me to a different school. I explained the situation, but she refused. She nonchalantly told me that I needed to work it out. I then told her I wanted to kill myself and had tried that afternoon with a fork. I think she laughed, telling me a fork wouldn't do any damage. I guess she must have perceived my troubles as normal school-age trials, but it turned out to be a missed warning sign of my self-destructive behavior to follow.

My mother had always put a lot of pressure on me to do well in school and to attend a university directly out of high school. She expected me to be at the top of everything I did. "I just want you to live up to your potential," she would say. This isn't a horrible thing for a parent to say, of course, but I was tired of trying to live up to *her* potential. How did she know how well I could do, and why wasn't it good enough to just be happy with doing things my way? No, it always had to be more, so much more that I felt every goal that was set was unattainable. Unfortunately, I had an intense desire to please both of my parents—actually, anybody I met. I never wanted to let anyone down. After a while, I began to take on the pressure on my own without anyone else even having to say anything. Eventually the pressure to be perfect became too much.

## TARA'S DIARY

### 1/22/86

*Well, today is the first day I am writing in here, and I am hoping I will save this and someday I will look back in here and enjoy it. First I will tell you about myself. I am 12 and in 7th grade. I have a cat—*

Frisky—3 dogs, Mish, Fuzzy, Sombra and a hamster—Ortho.

Today I had a good day. I wore something I like and it felt good.

I have my eye on some guys—Dan Hanson I know I will never get—Shawn Cox I think he might like me—Dennis—is a jerk sort of. My grandparents are visiting they are starting to bug me. -Bye-

**1/23/86**

I just came back from gymnastics and had a fight with my mom about it we're not speaking to each other. I hate fighting with my mom because I have too much to talk to her about!

I am feeling depressed because Angela is so much better than me in everything. Oh well. I still sort of like Shawn except he sort of brags a lot. Eric is ok too. I give an oral report tomorrow about crocheting. There is a dance at school tomorrow night I am going. -Bye-

**2/2/86**

I haven't written in here for a while so I will probably take up a lot! Today is my mom's birthday. She is 36. You wouldn't believe what has been happening to me. This guy named Sam. I started liking him about 1 week ago at a dance and then he liked me and we were like going together and just last Thursday he moved to Lancaster. I was so depressed because he was in 8th grade and is such a babe! We hugged good bye and I'm going to write to him. Jill is being a jerk lately Sally is being good. Wanda's being ok I guess. -Well Bye-

**6/5/86**

Today should have been a bad day cuz I got a referral—Mr. Burns is such a dick!!! My mom didn't even get mad I was so surprised!

Today I like Jeff again! I stopped liking him for a while cuz we got moved from each other—but I still think he's a total babe!

Even though that bitch Leanne likes him and he probably likes her!

My dad moved from Century City to San Fernando Valley a couple of days ago. I think I'm becoming closer to my dad—that's wonderful!

[Author's Note: My dad was working in Century City and commuting over an hour each way. He changed offices to the San Fernando Valley, which shortened his commute to 30 minutes. I was excited because I thought Dad would be home more and be less irritable from the traffic.]

### 12/28/86

It's right after Christmas. I got a TV yeah! I'm thinking of trying out for a play at school called Annie, but it's a musical which means I'd have to sing—bummer! For the audition I might sing Zip e dee do dah. Jill said she had a stiff neck today then she went home crying because of it what a baby!

My mom let me read her diary.

Gregg is moving out of the house to go to San Diego State University in June. I really don't want him to go—I'll miss him even though we fight a lot I still don't want him to go. He has a new girlfriend now her name is Darlene—she's really cool—she comes over a lot! He had a different one before named Tammy that's who he went to homecoming with. Bye!

### July 1st my birthday! "87"

Haven't been great about writing in here lately but I'm going to try to do better.

Today is my birthday, and it sucks! Jill wasn't even here to celebrate w/ me and I think my parents saw it as more of a hassle than anything else. They didn't even take the time to get me a present I wanted. They actually had the nerve to get me a pooper scooper for my b-day (it is my new chore to clean up the dog crap in the yard). They have to be the worst parents on earth!! -Bye-

### 8/1/87

Summer is going okay I don't want to go back to sucky school. I'm not excited to start high school I don't know why. I'm getting so fat these days I have to stop eating so much I'm not a kid anymore I can't eat like I used to. I hate my stomach there is this layer of fat over it. Mom says it's just skin or sometimes she calls it baby fat—I'm 14—it's not baby fat anymore—she is so lame! I've been swimming a lot— hopefully that will help me not get fat—but it makes me so hungry after workouts I don't know! -Bye-

### 8/26/87

Gregg left for college. I had no idea I would be this upset. I can't stop crying. I don't even know why—I hate him. He's been nothing but mean to me my entire life. I should be glad that he is not around here anymore to torture me. But I'm not. I'm lonely and sad.

Mom is so depressed. She's not even cooking her normal Sunday dinners. It's like our family is frozen in time. Everybody's walking around in a catatonic haze. Gregg gets to go off to San Diego to live his life. But our lives are not continuing. I don't want to be left here alone w/ mom and dad—or should I say, left here alone period? They are never home these days anyway. I get scared being in the house at night by myself. I hide in my bedroom under my blankets and wait for the sound of the garage door to open. When I hear one of them walk in I know I'm not alone anymore and I can finally fall asleep.

I'm sad sad sad sad sad!!!

**9/7/87**

School sucks. It's such a big change. There are so many more people—and they are all older. I feel so little walking thru the halls.

And the work is kinda tough. I dread going everyday. How am I going to last here for 4 yrs??

Oh well I have Jill and Wanda and we all just stick together.

I feel huge—swimming is not helping—maybe making it worse! Bye

## LINDA'S DIARY

### July 1, 1986

Tara's 13th birthday. Louie was in charge. He and Tara went to Solvang via motorcycle. We all went to dinner at Hungry Hunter. Tara got 13 loser lottery tickets and a pooper scooper!

### June 25, 1987

Tara began summer school this morning (8-12:30) after her morning swim workout. I took her at 5:45 AM (Jill didn't go this AM), picked her up at 1:35. She dressed in the car, we stopped at a gas station where she could comb her wet hair ("I look dumb mom"), then took her to her 1st H.S. class at TOHS. I'll go to Camarillo at 12:30, then go back to Camarillo for a client later in the day.

Louie has been feeling rotten physically—more emotionally.
We're probably both clinically depressed—the $ situation bothers us
both. Things are tighter now than any time since we 1st started (and
we have more obligations and greater expectations). Gregg doesn't
have a place to stay in San Diego yet . . . I was able to pay for the
truck and SDSU—nothing but enough to pay July 1 rent—oh well.

*July 2, 1987, Tara's Birthday*

Tara's birthday (14) yesterday—pretty lousy for a B'day—I'm
sure she will remember that, just like no gifts last year. She was
"down" and we knew nothing would change the fact that Jill was
gone, for the 2nd year in a row to Alaska to spend Holly's b'day.

Things just don't seem to be clicking around here lately. Our
family seems to be out of sync. I decided yesterday that I regret
getting into the field of psychotherapy and I wish I had just gotten a
two-year college degree, and gone to work for a company. By now I
would be working my way up to a decent wage. The price has been
too much, for my family, for me. I never thought I would think this
way.

Even if I got all my accounts receivable paid today it wouldn't
make up for the pain, the waiting, this family has had to endure. If I
knew then what I know now . . .

I still like counseling—but not the price I've (we've) had to pay.
Other jobs could have been rewarding too. Oh well—I'll have to
live with this one.

I don't know if I've ever been so worried about money—even in the old days—we didn't have the obligations, the expectations from others and ourselves then.

I have no $ in the checking account. $175.00 in savings and the rent check (for food) probably will take several days to get here, and July 4th weekend is here—and I'm going to lunch today—What do I tell my associates—I can't afford lunch? I'm supposed to be a "professional." The guilt and feelings I have for Louie are almost overwhelming—I have cost him so much and finally got to a place in life where I wanted to have fun, allow myself some pleasure, didn't feel bad about myself intrinsically anymore—and what do I get? More waiting—I'm sick of waiting—this stinks—Louie deserves better than this—having to be broke and live with a complaining depressed wife. Shit.

The pressure is incredible—and I know he feels it too—normally would be letting it out—he seems more patient than I. I think back on our marvelous discussions and planning and anticipation at Lake Tahoe in winter—seeing light at the end of the tunnel, feeling like I could finally contribute, give back and lessen Louie's pressure a little, feel good about giving to him and the kids.

This probably will pass, at least to this extreme—god I hope.


*August 27, 1987*

Gregg left for college Monday—today is Thursday. I couldn't write until now, as I have been a total emotional wreck over this. I knew it would be difficult, but not this much! I couldn't even say good-bye to him, as I was so choked-up and was trying not to cry— for his sake. Tara burst into tears when she saw his note on the bathroom mirror, "See ya Tara, love Gregg." She said, "I didn't think it would hurt so much." On top of all this, I guess I just feel too young to be going thru this, feel cheated—it went by too fast. I realized that in spite of all my ambition and working to get my degrees, and being so compulsive, being a mom is the only really important thing and what has been most meaningful to me—I probably haven't conveyed that feeling, but it's true.

It's so lonely here—Tara will be gone all too soon. I'm anticipating that and feeling bad already.

*October 12, 1987*

We've been renting lots of movies lately, doing yard and pool work. Lou and I were gone a lot last week—and Tara suffered and was angry because of it.

Tara and I decorated for Halloween today—that was fun. I'm cooking a roast for dinner. Louie says it's not good for us, but I feel the need to do some domestic-type things just to keep the sense of family alive—salads and pasta and diet foods just don't make it. It still hurts when I think of Gregg gone. I am already anticipating Tara leaving—I hope I can replace the time/effort and not look back too much. I tend to naturally hold on and mourn the past— perhaps I got that from my grandmother.

## TARA'S DIARY

*1/5/88*

I'm trying out for the swim team! I can't believe I'm doing this. I had to
go and pick the one sport that you have to wear a bathing suit in. If I
didn't love swimming so much I would never do this. But I always wear 2
or 3 suits so you can't see my body as much. I also take my towel right
to the pool edge and drop it right before I dive into the water. Most of
the girls on the team do this. We're all sooo self-conscious of our bodies.
Every day in the locker room you can hear almost every girl complain
about her body. At least we all have that in common. I HAVE TO STOP
EATING!! Dressing out every day is like pure hell for me. I think about it
all day. I don't know how I even focus on my schoolwork anymore.

I'm doing double workouts everyday now. I dive in the water @6
every morning and swim for about 1½ hours. Then after school we have
our team workout for 2½ hours. So I'm swimming like 4 hours every
day and I'm still fat. How can that be? What the hell do I have to do to
look the way I want to look? I'm cutting down my meals. I stopped
eating breakfast and I eat a bag of Cheetos and a candy bar for lunch
every day and that's it. But then I am so hungry after the afternoon
workout that I go home and eat a lot. I don't know how to stop eating. I
am not strong enough. I need to get stronger so I can change the image
in the mirror. Because right now, I HATE THE WAY I LOOK!

*2/16/88*

I feel so stressed out right now. I am so sick of everyone talking
about college—like it's the most important thing in the whole entire
world. My mom will not shut up about it. Every move I make these days

somehow relates to college. Why can't I just do the things that I want to do instead of everything being such an issue? If I say anything about swim team, my mom always has a comment about how great swimming will look on my college apps. And if it's not my mom, then it's the teachers and counselors. And god forbid I choose not to go to college. I don't even have a choice in my own future. It's just always been told to me that I would be going to college. I'm trying my best. And I'm getting really frustrated because the A's aren't coming to me as easily as they used to. And I have to get A's if I'm going to keep my GPA up high enough to get into a good school. Ahhhh!

### 3/19/88

I got the chicken pox! They were sooo bad, I couldn't even write in here. And of course I got them from my dumb brother who came home from college with them—another way he has added to making my life a living hell. I'm too old to have the chicken pox. I wish my stupid mom had gotten me exposed to them when I was a little kid. I have scars all over my body and face. I look so ugly. I had them everywhere—and I mean EVERYWHERE! They were in places I didn't even know I had.

Mom finally went through the house and covered all the mirrors with sheets cuz everytime I walked by a mirror I started to cry. I guess it was nice of her to do that—she has been pretty good about understanding my feelings. Probably cuz she can plainly see how ugly I am right now. Why did god do this to me? What have I done to deserve this? Like I didn't hate the way I looked before—now I just want to die!

### 3/22/88

I got a puppy! I was down the street playing @ Jill's and dad called me and said come home you have chores to do. I was so pissed off. I already picked up the dog shit but I walked up the street and into the house. I knew something was going on cuz mom and dad were just standing there looking @ the laundry basket filled w/ clothes. They said come over here and fold the clothes before you go back to Jill's house. My heart started to flutter cuz I just knew there had to be something good in the basket. My parents have always been so good about surprising me w/ things. It makes me feel so important when they take the time to plan out a scheme. I bent down to the basket and lifted off the top layer of clothes and inside was a tiny black fur ball. I named her Samantha and she is the 1st thing that has made me smile in weeks! Mom and dad can sure shock me sometimes, just when I think they are the worst people I've ever known, they go and make me love them again.

### 4/19/88

I'm getting tired of writing in here. I hope my dad gets the computer soon. He's getting one from Xerox—it's gonna be so cool—then I can type on it—mom said I can use it whenever I want.

Today was so much fun. This guy that Jill and I have been hanging around more lately—Nathan—asked us if we wanted a ride after school. He has this super nice 4x4 truck—it is so cool. So we got in with him and he took us mud womping. We went driving around the hills near the high school where it was all muddy from the rain yesterday. We were bouncing around the cab like crazy. I was so scared. He drives like a maniac. But it was also a lot of fun. Except that when I was getting out of his truck I leaned against the side of it and got my new white Guess jeans all full of mud. I'm so pissed. And I didn't know how I was going to explain that to mom. But I had plenty of time to soak, wash and dry them before she got home. It's 9:15 and she's still not home. I could do anything I want and never get caught around this house. My parents have no idea what I do when they are not home. They are so stupid. See ya-

**5/11/88**

Yeah my dad finally got the computer so I probably won't be writing in here anymore.

I can't wait til I get my driver's license so I can have more freedom.

Mom and dad have this stupid rule about no driving in cars with boys—like they are gonna attack me on the way home from school or something.

But it makes it pretty difficult to get around this town—all my friends drive in cars with boys. It's so unfair cuz it's not like I have a lot of options—they are never here to drive me anywhere.

**5/20/88**

I dig this new computer. Typing is so much better than writing things out. Although I'm not very good at typing yet, so it's taking me a while cuz I have to keep going back and correcting things. But it's still fun. I'm so glad school is almost over. I can't wait for summer. I want to lay out and get all tan. But I dread the thought of a bikini right now. I am so fat.

**6/1/88**

My birthday is in 1 month. How much you wanna bet I get another pooper scooper. Maybe a new and improved model . . . what a joke. I hate my birthday. It always seems like a big hassle for everyone. Sometimes I wish I was never born. I think my family would like it better that way.

**6/11/88**

Summer is going well. I've been hanging with Jill a lot. We are like such good friends now. I pretty much live at her house. I like her family. Her mom doesn't work and is always home—sometimes she bugs us but I like it. And her dad comes home from work at like 5:30. They have dinner together every night. They have pretty much just included me as part of their family—they don't even ask anymore, they just assume that I'm going to eat over and be there all the time.

**7/1/88**

Another birthday down. And it sucked again . . . what a surprise! I'm just glad it's over with—I've been such a bitch all month. I get so crazy right before my birthday. I don't know why. I just feel so bratty and spoiled. I feel guilty for wanting the things I want for my b-day. Mom says we can't afford the stuff I want so I feel so shitty for being mad about that.

**8/15/88**

Back to school soon. Yuck. And I need clothes and cute stuff to start the year off right. My mom is being so stingy about everything. All my friends are getting such cool stuff. Jill's mom gets her whatever she asks for it's so unfair.

**8/24/88**

I got the leather jacket I wanted! But my stupid parents made me pay for it, of course. They are so unreasonable, they don't understand that I neeeeeeed these things. Everybody else at school has them, and I'm sure they didn't have to pay for them on their own. I don't know *why they insist on making life more difficult for me. Like paying for the jacket is going to make me a more financially responsible human being—give me a break.*

### 9/1/88

*I hate going back to school, but this year was not as bad as last. At least we're not the youngest ones on campus anymore. I'm going to Palm Springs with Jill and her family. It's going to be so much fun cuz Brian is bringing Matt Brown—who I think I might like. Should be a fun weekend.*

### 9/10/88

*Palm Springs was soooo much fun. Jill and I took her dad's new t-bird and went cruising the strip. These hot guys on motorcycles would come driving up and ask us if we wanted a ride. I wanted to go so bad, but I didn't want to leave Jill. So we stuck together. Nothing happened with Matt. He was a jerk—he and Brian met some other girls and they hung out with them. But I didn't care cuz Jill and I had our own fun. I felt so good this weekend, all tan and I've lost a little weight so I think I was not a total huge whale.*

## LINDA'S DIARY

*January 6, 1988*

Tara seems more withdrawn these days—sometimes she almost seems depressed. I know that can't be. She has always been such a happy child. There isn't anything going on around her that would make her upset. I must just be imagining the sadness? I think things will be getting better soon. I hope. Tara tried out for the swim team yesterday. She is such a good swimmer. I hope she sees the value of such activities, especially for her college transcripts. It seems like a great activity. There will be a lot of traveling and time spent practicing. She has such talent!

I wish I had such opportunities when I was her age. I wish her the best!

*March 17, 1988*

Brought Samantha (puppy) home for Tara. She's sleeping now—memories of when the kids were young.

*March 18, 1988*

Today was Tara's 2nd day back from school after having the chicken pox—14 days after Gregg came home with them. She had a much worse case—more pox and lasting longer—at a lousy age. She was teased at school yesterday—had a lousy day. She missed the 1st several swim meets also.

. . . Tara came home from school with her friends in a boy's car—against our rules to date. I thought this might be of interest in future years—as she goes thru this with her kids—she did tell us this time—thinks we are far too strict (of course).

*April 19, 1988*

While I'm sitting here wondering where Tara is I guess I'll write catch-up notes.

She got out early from school today and is probably out driving around with friends or ? I thought she'd be here and possibly need a ride. Oh, well . . .

Tara was in an invitational swim meet in Simi all day Sat.—she'd done good locally but not pleased in the larger meet. She and Jill are constantly at odds over swimming—very competitive with each other and having different values. . . .

*August 24, 1988*

We bought the leather jacket the other day that Tara wanted—$200 (she paid $90). I'm sure she will remember she paid all or most of it. She put $10 plus a car wash toward her $60 tennis shoes too. She also found a semi-formal (green, strapless) for $80 that we decided was a bargain and put it on layaway.

*October 16, 1988*

Tara just left with Alex and some kid to drive to Oxnard and the mall—parent nightmare! We're giving her a hard time but this is scary!

Homecoming is next week and she says she's not going—oh well.

She got 2 referrals from school—Geometry and Spanish II. We've got a tutor for her—no results yet.

She is training Samantha in doggie school—every Wed. night for 10 weeks. She's also swimming 5 days per week—busy girl.

I came home unexpectedly last week and found Alex and friend in the house against our rules of no boys in the house. I guess he's lucky to be alive let alone still allowed to see her. They walked to Jill's house to get pizza Friday night. She has only been talking to him for about 1½ weeks.

*October 20, 1988*

Big fuss last night as I was called by Alex's (homecoming date) parents who were concerned about the kids' plans, especially limo $. Tara of course became angry with me, them, etc. "All their plans are ruined—they might as well not go." We'll see . . .

*October 31, 1988*

Halloween.

Tara and Jill just went out to trick or treat—punk rocker and bat lady. Tara kept getting calls from Alex who wanted to come over and go out with them. She's trying to discourage him—decided she doesn't like him.

*November 7, 1988*

Gregg came home—we didn't see much of him (surfing), but it was nice to have him home. I think Tara got a little jealous of all the attention paid to him . . .

I get so excited at the precious moments when we all feel like family—when Gregg picks his sister up and she says "stop it"—but I can tell that now she doesn't really mean it (different than when they were little)—or waking Gregg up Sunday AM with the dogs jumping on his bed and Lou walking in with shaving creme on his face—or Gregg coming home from surfing and jumping on Tara's bed and tickling her—or all of us just playing with the dogs—nice times, nice memories.

## TARA'S DIARY

### 12/26/88

*Been busy lately. Haven't had a lot of time to write. But I'm getting so much better at typing. I'm going to take a typing class next semester so I can get even better. Christmas was good. The usual stuff. Mom and dad always go all out on Christmas. They do such a good job of getting us stuff and making it fun. They still leave our big present (the one from Santa) by the fireplace every xmas morning. And mom still fills everyone's stockings. She still denies that she does any of it. We all just play along with her. She doesn't really think we still believe in Santa, does she? Oh well, it's fun anyway. The dinner she made was so good. I love turkey and mashed potatoes and stuff. Now 2 months in a row of pigging out. I feel so sick after I eat like that. I wish I could just go and throw it up afterwards.*

## LOOKING BACK

## TARA

During my preadolescence, I distinctly remember feeling viciously torn between wanting to remain a little girl and wanting to have the independence of a teenager. Inside I wanted to be nurtured like a young child, yet outside I looked like a capable young woman ready to take on the world. It is no wonder my parents didn't recognize my impending inner turmoil.

Even though I was nearly a teenager, I still longed for my mother's attention. And the more she became committed to her new career, the more I felt I needed her at home with me. Seeing her light up as she marveled in the triumphs of her workday made me fearful that she would leave me altogether. Yet, not truly understanding or accepting this fear, I channeled my anxiety and doubt into an emotion I was familiar with—anger.

However, negative emotions were not "acceptable" in my house. I didn't feel safe expressing anger outwardly, so I began to channel it inwardly. And because it was easier to believe that the intense pain I felt was attributed to my appearance rather than deeply embedded emotional issues, I directed my self-doubt toward the image I saw in the mirror.

In the midst of my battle to identify an acceptable self-concept, my physical body was taking new shape. The so-called "natural" pubescent development of my body seemed startlingly unnatural to me. I felt powerless to control the kind of woman I was turning into, which only fueled my need to discover something that I thought I could control—food.

## LINDA

Even over a decade later, it is both painful and embarrassing for me to read some of Tara's diary entries. At the time, my daughter was very capable and did not appear to need me much. She was so good at making it look like she didn't need me—yet all the time telling her diary how I had abandoned her. I remember thinking everything was going great because Tara was active and involved in school and extracurricular activities. Because Tara was not coming home with purple hair and strange tattoos, I believed she was happy and healthy. She and I had our battles, but for the most part we got along well during this time. As I've seen with my clients, but overlooked in my own home, too often the kids who seem "perfect" are the ones who are truly in trouble. Because I was wrapped up in my own personal struggles, I wanted desperately to believe that she was okay and always would be.

However, over the next year, I could no longer fool myself. It became clear that my communication with Tara had completely broken down. It came to a point where it seemed the only way I could reach her was by telling her stories, which were loosely based upon those my grandmother told to me. These brief metaphorical "bunny stories," which they became known as, told of forest animals facing difficult, seemingly impossible challenges, yet somehow finding the courage from within to triumph. In a desperate attempt to save my daughter, they served as a sort of rope being thrown down for her to grab on to.

## CHAPTER 3, SPRING AND SUMMER 1989
## EXPERIMENTING WITH PURGING
*"How could a mother not know the terrible things her daughter was doing?"*

As trite as it seems, the genesis of my eating disorder was an innocent competition between my dad and me. I was 16 and at the beginning of my junior year of high school. Dad would come home from work and eat a large meal, then spend the next hour complaining about how much he ate and how fat he was. He would say he was weak for eating. At the time, he was unaware that he was channeling his anxiety and depression into his ritualistic eating. My dad now recognizes that he had disordered eating habits. As a man, this concept was difficult for him to accept. He, like many others, believed body image and eating disorders were solely a female concern. He inadvertently taught me how to have a love-hate relationship with food. And we had found something we had in common—self-hate. It became a nightly ritual for us to bond over complaints about food intake and body size.

One night my dad had the idea that we would have a competition to see who could lose the most weight. Dad and I were constantly debating or challenging each other in some way. It seemed like a great idea. The desire to win and please my dad with my superior willpower quite logically led me to an eating disorder. Yet,

I believe I would have developed the disorder regardless of whether we started the contest. It just pushed things along faster. I was searching for a way to cope with my fear and anxiety. I was also compulsively focused on the shape of my body. Restricting and purging were the magic tools that helped me deal with both.

I became attached to purging very quickly. Each time I threw up, I fell more in love with the high it gave me. It became an obsession I thought about all the time. I held the unattainable goal of being able to live without food. I truly believed I could survive on nothing.

Despite the unhealthy eating patterns I was developing, my life in school was fairly normal at this time. From the outside I looked like your basic teenage girl, focused on getting good grades and having fun. Inside I was experiencing a tremendous amount of anxiety about getting into college, which to me meant the difference between winning my parents' love and losing it. I was preparing for the SATs. My pre-SAT scores were, well, less than glowing. My mom said they did not accurately reflect my intelligence. I was afraid that they did indeed reflect my intelligence and I had just been fooling everyone all these years.

## TARA'S DIARY

### 3/16/89

Dad told me that grandpa has cancer. I've never seen my dad cry before and it is scary to watch him deal with this. He is so sad. He hasn't laughed since we found out. It's like the end of the world around here. I don't understand what everybody's so worried about. He's going to be just fine . . . right?

I'm so miserable I can't even think straight. I hate everything. I hate my parents. I hate the way I look. I am so fat. I started these classes to become a lifeguard and I can barely get through the classes because I'm so distracted by how bad I look in a bathing suit. I can't even believe I'm allowing anybody to see me in these ugly suits with all my fat sticking out everywhere. I wouldn't go through this if I didn't want to teach swimming so bad.

**3/18/89**

Mom made me sit with her and watch this stupid Peter, Paul and Mary reunion show on TV. What a joke! Does she really think that is music? She is so lame!

**4/3/89**

Grandpa died today. I had a swim meet at the high school. I saw my Dad come in the pool area and I was so excited. I thought he came to watch me swim. But as he walked closer to me, I realized he would never leave work in the middle of the day just to watch me swim. He told me about Grandpa and I started to cry and told him I wanted to go home with him, I didn't want to stay and swim my races. And he told me I had to stay—that I was part of the team and I had a responsibility to fulfill. I can't believe he did that to me. How could he not understand how I felt? I barely finished my races. I was swimming through the water with tears coming out of my eyes. And now they are going to leave me and go to Connecticut for the funeral without me. But who cares, I don't want to go deal with all that crap anyway.

**4/6/89**

I miss mom and dad. I hate this. I don't even have my brother to be sad with. Just me all alone. Alone alone alone.

**5/12/89**

Been boring around here. I hope something exciting happens this summer. I'm sick of my life. Nothing good ever happens to me. I got a job at the TO YMCA. My mom actually saw the job advertised in the paper. I'm so glad she did cuz I think it's gonna be pretty fun. I love kids so much, so I'm so glad I get to work with them.

I'm really nervous about having to be in a bathing suit all the time. Chris (my boss) said I can't wear shorts or anything over in case I need to jump in to save a little kid. Makes sense I guess, but I don't care if I get my shorts wet. I'd drench my whole wardrobe if it meant I didn't have to show my body. I might as well be naked.

**5/15/89**

I haven't been sleeping well. I keep having dreams about going to school and getting my books out of my locker and then I look down and notice that I don't have ANY clothes on. Then I look up and see the whole school looking at me and laughing. I don't know if I can do this. Maybe I should quit the job . . . before I even start.

**5/23/89**

I really like my job. I love being with the kids. The baby classes are my favorite. Except I have to sing dumb songs and I have a terrible voice. But the babies are so cute. And the whole bathing suit thing is not that big a deal. I tie my jacket around my waist to cover my stomach and ass and those are really the only parts I care about. So I'm fine with it. Thank god—I was so stressed about it. There is this one guy at work who is really cute. He is a lot older than me though—he's in college!!!

### 6/13/89

I have never been so happy in all my life! I have fallen in love and I feel like I am walking on air. My parents do not know yet so I will not even write his name down in this journal, in case someone peeks. I have so much energy to do things. I am just sure I am going to marry this man. He makes me so happy. This is the best summer I have ever had. I'm doing what I love—teaching swimming to kids. I am in the warm sun all day. And I look okay—I am tan and thinner. I have not been eating barely at all lately. I have constant butterflies in my stomach that make me not hungry, which is great because I'm trying to stay thin to look good for my new love. I hope I can keep not eating. What if I get fat? He'll probably break up with me. I know guys like skinny girls. I have to make sure I stay that way!

### 7/2/89

Yesterday was my sweet 16. It was the best birthday I've ever had. For the first time in my life, my parents gave me exactly what I wanted for my birthday. Normally I ask for a new bike and get a pooper-scooper! But this year I asked my mom to let me get acrylic nails and some clothes and to let me stay out past my curfew. And they actually listened to me!

### 7/20/89

My stupid parents made me go camping with them last weekend. They don't realize that I don't want to be around them anymore. I want to see Mitch and spend time with him. I think about him all the time and I missed him so much this weekend. But of course I can't tell them that because they don't even know about Mitch. I know I have to tell them soon . . . but I'm scared.

## 8/1/89

Well, I did it. I told my mom about Mitch. And just as I expected she freaked out. All it took was for me to tell her how old he is and without waiting for me to tell her anything else about him, she forbid me to see him. I was so shocked I couldn't even speak. How could she forbid me from the only thing bringing me any happiness in life? I am convinced she is on this earth to make my life miserable. Well I don't give a shit what she says, I am not going to stop seeing him. He loves me and I love him. Nobody can keep us apart.

## 8/10/89

I haven't felt like writing as much lately. I don't know why. I'm not too happy about what I've been doing lately. It started a few months ago, but I haven't wanted to write about it. I guess I didn't want to admit it was really happening. I wanted to pretend that things were going along just fine. But the truth is they haven't been.

I don't even really know why this has started—I was lying in bed and I just ate this huge dinner. I was feeling really full and fat, so I went into the bathroom and tried to throw up. To my surprise, it worked. The first time I vomited very little came up, but I was proud of myself, proud because I had control of the food. I also didn't feel as fat afterward. The next day I threw up two more times and two times every day for about a week after that. During that first week I felt so in control and almost better than everybody else, better that is, except for people thinner than me.

I want to share my new discovery with my friends and my mom who I tell most everything to. The other night I asked Kyla if she had ever tried throwing up her food. She said that she had tried it a long time ago, but it didn't really work. I really want to tell someone about this, I feel like it's eating away at me.

**8/16/89**

I didn't sleep with mom last night like I normally do when dad is out of town. She made me so mad. She isn't even trying to understand how I feel about Mitch. Which is such bullshit because she met dad when she was 18 and got pregnant before they were married. The first time mom took dad to meet her parents was when she told them she was pregnant. At least I'm not doing that. I don't see what the big deal is about our ages. It is only a number. She of all people should know that I am very mature for my age. It would be ridiculous for me to date a boy my own age because boys mature later than girls do anyway.

**8/25/89**

Last night I asked my mom some questions about bulimia and anorexia, like what throwing up did to your teeth and what problems it could cause your body. I thought that for sure she would know what I was doing to myself. How could a mother not know the terrible things her daughter was doing?

**8/26/89**

I went almost the whole day without eating today. I was so proud of myself. Then at around 8:00 tonight I broke down and ate a piece of bread. So then, of course, I had to throw it up. I am so disappointed in myself. If I could have lasted the whole day without eating, then I would have been able to go a whole day without throwing up.

**8/27/89**

I only ate 4 bites of cereal and 2 bites of banana today. Not too bad I guess. So I only had to throw up once. I'm so tired tonight. I got up at 5 to do my morning swim workout, then swam again for 2 hours after school. And I went to aerobics tonight as usual, but I rode my bike there and back. I didn't realize how far it was—I think like 10 miles each way. I'm just going to fall into bed. I feel so weak. My energy sucks these days!

**8/29/89**

When I talked to my mom last week, I was surprised that she answered my questions so calmly. I assumed she forgot about it. Then today I started feeling guilty and scared. I thought to myself you're a therapist's daughter and you're so educated about these things you could never get caught up in this. Because of my guilty conscious I told my mom tonight that I hadn't been having very good eating habits lately. She immediately asked if I had been making myself throw up. I wanted so badly to tell her, but I didn't want her to yell at me. So I didn't say anything. Probably figuring my silence proved my guilt, she responded with I can't believe this Tara, this is a problem.

I tried to calm her down, but I was unsuccessful. She dragged me into my parents' room to tell my father. He seemed to take it well, just joking about it and acting like it was no big deal. That pissed mom off even more. I am just dreading life now. Mom is going to be watching every meal I eat. I should have never said anything to her. This is going to become a nightmare.

## LINDA'S DIARY

*Sunday, March 5, 1989*

We found out Thursday that Lou's dad has cancer. Things have, of course, been highly stressful this week. I got a call last Saturday that my dad was still ill after an accident a month ago.

Tara had her first swim meet, but I guess it didn't go well. I haven't heard much about it, but then there is a lot going on. She's been going through a lot too—worries about her friends and others and Jill and Brian with marijuana. She has had no "loves" for quite a while—life's been pretty boring and stressful for her this year so far. With our $ worries, I'm sure that adds to her as well—she wants a car, clothes—but of course are out of the question for now.

*March 10, 1989*

Louie left for the airport today. He is going to visit his father and family. We don't know how bad the cancer is, but his dad seems to be feeling OK. Now that I look back, last Christmas when his parents were here, his dad was complaining about being cold all the time. It irritated me—how could he be cold when they live in the snow? This should have been a hint to me that something was wrong! I am so thick in the head sometimes.

### March 11, 1989

Louie called again, everyday, of course. I'm glad he's spending time with his father. He says he's going with him to the doctor tomorrow. I mowed the lawn today. This is hard work! Gregg isn't here to do it and Lou is gone. I miss him but I know this is important.

Louie is in Conn. with his parents—things don't sound good. Sally came over this morning to tell me to think again about going with him. We've gotten lots of support from my colleagues.

Tara started Advanced Lifesaving today—1–5:30—she was in such a lousy mood when done too! Grump Grump!

### Sunday, March 12, 1989, 5:30 PM

Tara is at Jill's—I just took a shower—feels great. I've been refinishing the dining room chairs all weekend—I had to have a project you know. My stomach feels lousy, I got a headache after talking with Louie and his family—he says things are "worse than you can imagine."

Tara drove to Camarillo (In-N-Out Burger) today (that probably contributed to my headache also). She merged into a car and in front of a CHP [California Highway Patrol]! Oh dear. She did finally get into 5th gear though!

*Tuesday, March 14, 1989*

Louie's dad is on the way to the ER to have the fluid taken out of his lungs. Louie says he's much worse just since he arrived Friday.

Today it's warm and sunny—wish I could work outside all day. Tara swam at 5:45 am. I went back to bed.

*March 15, 1989*

Louie called, he doesn't know what to do. He wants to stay in Conn. with his dad, but he has a job he needs to come home to. It sounds like he has really connected with his father during this time. He seems to be in agony about the decision to stay there or come home. The doctors say now that there is not much time for his dad to live . . . but how much time? He can't stay there and be gone from home too long. We have a life here too. I can't tell him what to do, this is too important. I did a difficult thing by sitting down to write a letter to his dad, a good-bye letter. I have talked to him on the phone, but I can't say certain things on the phone. I am going to miss him—he's a good man.

*March 17, 1989*

The 25th anniversary Peter, Paul and Mary concert is on TV. Tara says it is boring and I told her that in 25 years when she wants to listen to Tiffany, Madonna, the Bangles, etc and her kids say it is dumb she'll say OK—oh sure—we'll see.

*April 3, 1989*

Lou's father died today—I think this is the first time I ever saw Lou sob.

RIP Louis Joseph Rio, Sr.

*Monday, April 10, 1989*

Lou's father died Monday April 3, 1989. We got back yesterday. Now back to dealing with reality—sounds funny—we've been dealing with the ultimate reality.

*June 12, 1989*

Tara is driving me crazy! Yuck—teenagers—the shit has changed just since Jill got her license—instantly! Louis brings home his sport bike tonight.

*June 14, 1989*

It's strange. She actually seems to be happy today—lately too. I'm not quite sure why, but it's a nice change. She seems to have so much more energy and enthusiasm about life. I think she is really enjoying her job—teaching swimming. Whatever it is that's causing this new attitude, I hope it stays.

*July 2, 1989*

Tara's 16th birthday—she got home at 1:25—later curfew as a "gift." She takes her driving test at 9:00 AM Monday.

Gregg is home!

*July 21, 1989*

Oh, let's see—we went camping to Hunington Lake (SP?)last weekend—Tara, Jill (and Lou) gave me lots of hard times about going. Tara has been a real pain ever since Jill turned 16—things have changed!! This is worse than diapers and 3:00 AM feedings! We have no idea (or worse, some idea) of what she is out there doing—we have to let go but how much and when?? I'm mostly (all) worried about the other people etc. She won't understand this until she is a mom.

*Sunday, August 6, 1989*

Tara drove to a Joanne Watley (spell?) concert at Universal Amphitheater on Thurs. I was (Lou and I) nervous—but of course she did just fine. She and I had a nice talk and that helped.

All in all it's been a pretty good summer—nice weather. Weekends have been busy with fun activities. Lou and I have discovered going out to the movies again—even staying out late.

*August 15, 1989 (9:35 PM)*

Tara just left the bedroom to sleep in her room (Louie is out of town on business) because, "I don't understand" about her feelings for Mitch (AKA 21-year-old).

*August 15, 1989*

Tara seems so stressed-out and worked-up over starting school this year. I have tried to tell her how important her junior year is for college. She will need to get the college applications off soon. I wish she had a clearer vision of where she wanted to go and a passion for a place or something. I wish I had known what I wanted at that age. I wish I had someone to guide me into a particular field. Lou's working late. I've been busy.

*August 25, 1989*

Tara approached me last night. She asked me a lot of weird questions. She scares me. I hope I answered her questions. I like it when she talks to me, but I don't know sometimes if she just wants to talk about just anything or whether it means something more. She hates me so much right now for not being here for her all the time. I can't seem to be able to reach her. I am working a lot this week and don't get to see her much during the week.

My practice is getting busier all the time, but I still worry a lot about keeping things going from a business side. I didn't realize how hard it would be to do all the paperwork and things necessary to keep this business going. It takes so much time! I worry all the time about whether I am doing the business part right. Yet, I know I have to keep that separate when I am in the room with clients. I can do that at the time, but after the anxiety hits. I so very much want to make my family proud of me, and not resent all the years of schooling they had to endure. God, I hate this pressure!

*August 26, 1989*

Gregg left to go back to SD. We went to dinner last night for his 20th birthday.

Tara's last day of work at the YMCA—quite a summer for her. She took a friend to the Public Health Clinic for a VD check yesterday.

Louie is on vacation—goes into work tomorrow (Sunday) and Monday (as part of vacation). No plans for the rest of it. All in all it has been a pretty good summer.

Tara has been acting strange lately, more withdrawn. She doesn't share as many things with me as she used to. I feel our close bond slipping away. Who am I kidding? It has been slipping away for a while. But I'm sure it's simply a stage she is going through right now.

*August 28, 1989*

It is 2:00 a.m. I couldn't sleep, so I guess I might as well do something. My whole life I have had sleepless nights. At least I don't walk in my sleep anymore. That used to freak my mom out.

Today is Gregg's 20th birthday! I never imagined myself having a 20-year-old child. He is away at school, of course. We never celebrate his actual birthday at home anymore because school always starts just around this time each year. Whatever happened to starting school after Labor Day? That's the way it used to be.

Louie's been busy at work, of course. I have too. I always feel pulled, when will that go away? I thought that once the kids got older and I went to work it would get easier. I am so tired of feeling guilty all the time! When I am at work I think I should be at home. When I am at home I think about all the paperwork to do at the office.

Tara seems fine these last few days. The questions she asked me the other night scared me. But now I think she was just curious. Maybe one of her friends is having a problem with something. She is so educated about these issues—sometimes I think too educated. I remember how proud I used to be when she would take my Marriage and Family Therapy magazines and read them from cover to cover. She has such a talent for understanding complex mental health issues. I hope that will protect her.

*Labor Day 1989*

Tara is still in Palm Springs with the Tanners. Louie and I decided (as part of our new life) to go near San Luis Obispo Sat. (he's always talking about that area). We went windsurfing at Castaic on the way back.

I called my mom today—so much negative when it comes to people. I wish I had more feelings for her—I guess she's been burned so is angry in return—I'm part of that even if she'd never say it.

It still feels sad having the kids gone—we're in transition now— parts feel good—doing things we've never really done—but if I were to have my choice I'd choose to have kids, family around.

## LOOKING BACK

## TARA

My grandfather's death had a profound effect on my family. My earliest memories of my Grandpa Rio, the patriarch of the family, are of a loud, gruff man who smelled like cigarettes pinching my cheeks so hard I would cry. Even though he and my grandma lived on the other side of the country, they always seemed close to our hearts. They usually came to visit once a year, which never seemed like enough to me. The son of Italian immigrants, my grandfather grew up poor. He joined the Army and ended up in the middle of WWII. He was captured by the Japanese and held in a POW camp for over 3 years. By the time he was rescued, irreparable damage had been done. He was constantly nervous and agitated and had violent nightmares. But because he had survived so much, he seemed invincible.

After my grandpa's death, there was a cloud of sadness that hung over our house for many months. My dad seemed empty, distracted, and less fulfilled. He held his father in great esteem, and when he died it seemed like a little piece of my dad died with him.

I wish I had gone to my grandpa's funeral. Instead, I was left home alone to grieve by myself. I had never lost anyone close to me before, and I didn't know how to do that. It took me years to process the grief that should have emerged back then.

By now, I associated all my problems with fat. This was much easier than trying to delve into them to analyze what they were really about. I truly believed that if I gained weight, Mitch would break up with me. Mitch never said anything to lead me to believe he felt my weight was an issue. In fact, he used to constantly tell me how beautiful I was and how much he loved my body. Yet despite this, I continued to channel all my fears of abandonment and rejection into something I could control—the size of my body.

The eating disorder began as a way to control my life. Admitting I had a problem meant I had to give up that control, at least for a little while. It also meant admitting that I was a failure (or at least I thought so back then). I felt as though the perfect daughter I was desperately trying to be had somehow turned into a sick, horrible, embarrassing child.

## LINDA

It was only years later that I realized the true impact that Lou's father's death had upon our family, especially Tara. I can see now that it was a mistake to try and shield them from the pain instead of letting them grieve and honor their grandfather.

I don't want to admit it, but I knew then that Tara was in trouble. I never consciously thought she had an eating disorder, at least early on, but I had known for a long time that we all were in trouble. I kept hoping we'd get through this phase and it would all be fine. She and I did have some good times that would give me a glimmer of hope in between the weeks of quiet battles. It took so much to open my eyes and get my attention. I think I was helpless to make the necessary changes alone, so I had to have my own daughter come to the brink of death in order to regain a healthy life.

## CHAPTER 4, EARLY FALL 1989
## A DOWNWARD SPIRAL
### *"I cannot believe what just happened tonight."*

One of the most dangerous aspects of my eating disorder was the overwhelming need to keep my disease a secret. At first I was in denial. I believed that I had control over what I ate and how many times I threw up. I thought I could stop at any time. There came a point, though, when I realized that I couldn't control my fast spiral downhill. But even then I wasn't ready to give up my coping mechanism. I became paranoid that someone would find out and make me stop. Having to hide this secret from the people I cared about was one of the most painful parts of the disease. I wanted to reach out to my mom for help, but I was afraid she wouldn't respond and I would end up more wounded. I was also consumed with anger, which acted as a solid wall blocking me from connecting with her.

When my parents did find out about my illness, I felt a mixture of trepidation and relief. I was scared that they would make me stop and I would get fat and become more depressed. But I was also relieved that my mom took the matter so seriously. It showed me that she was concerned about my well-being and committed to helping me feel better.

I also wanted to share this vital part of my life with Mitch. I wanted him to know how much pain I was in. I wanted him to nurture me and take that pain away. Ultimately, I wanted Mitch to save me from myself. But when I gently hinted about my "bad eating habits," he reacted angrily. He was understandably concerned about my health and didn't know how to help me. My relationship with him served as validation that I was desired and worthy of love, which is why the thought of it ending drove me to the brink of my depression.

During this time, I remember feeling torn between wanting to nurture my swimming talent and wanting to die rather than be seen in a swimsuit. I battled with this inner dilemma until my junior year of high school, when my self-loathing won out and I quit the swim team just after being named captain of the varsity team. The idea of even more people watching me compete with this new status drove me to give up the one thing I felt I did well. I went from a lifestyle where I burned an enormous amount of calories through my daily workouts to a more sedentary one. This drastic shift created a deeper sense of paranoia about weight gain and more free time to feel it. The adrenaline was noticeably absent from my life, leading me to find a new way to achieve the rush I used to feel from swimming.

**9/4/89**

Last night was a disaster. I had dinner with mom and dad. I ate a small meal then went into the bathroom and threw it up like normal. They assumed I kept it down and I went out and watched a movie with them. When I was getting ready for bed my mom came in to say goodnight, but first she went into the bathroom and found my dinner in the toilet. I guess it didn't flush all the way down. She came into my room and asked if I had vomited. I had a feeling she must have known, so I just smiled and said, yeah mom a little, it's no big deal. I'll never forget the look on her face. It showed anger, pain and worst of all disappointment.

Once again she dragged me in to tell my dad. This time he wasn't so nonchalant. My mom told me she was finding me some help. I guess I'm lucky to have parents that care as much as they do, although right now I wish they didn't care so much.

### 9/8/89

Yesterday I went to see an eating disorders specialist up in Santa Barbara. It was pretty cool because I didn't have to go to school. But mom had to miss work and it seemed like she was really mad at me all day.

The doctor diagnosed me with [anorexia and bulimia]. Basically, I eat very little food and whatever I do eat I throw up. The doctor kind of scared me. He said that this is the most dangerous kind of eating disorder because I'm not letting my body get any nutrients whatsoever. When he examined me he said that my throat was red and burned. He said my teeth were beginning to lose their enamel from the vomiting. He did an EKG (I think) and said that my heart was not functioning like it was supposed to. He said the constant throwing up was straining my heart—but I think he's making that up. How could throwing up affect your heart? He also said I had gastrointestinal-something or other. I think he was just trying to scare me . . . and it may have worked.

### 9/22/89

My mom just called from work. She said she made me another appointment with the doctor in Santa Barbara that specializes in "this

*sort of thing." She can't even bring herself to say it she's so disappointed.
I know she's embarrassed too. What a bitch. I'm the one in pain and
all she can think about is what effect this will have on her reputation in
the community.*

*I really don't see why I need to go to any doctor anymore anyway.
There isn't anything wrong with me. I need to do what I am doing in
order to keep in shape. I wish everyone would just leave me alone.
Yesterday I told Kyla and Jill about what I have been doing. I thought
they would understand. We always diet together and talk about all the
parts of our body that we would like to change. Instead of being
supportive of me they completely went over the deep end. They yelled
at me and told me I was going to hurt my body by what I was doing. I
don't know what they are talking about. I am just trying an extreme
diet. I have to diet like this. If I don't, Mitch won't want to go out with
me anymore. All guys like thin girls. So I don't care what everyone is
saying—I know I'm doing what I have to for myself.*

## LINDA'S DIARY

*September 4, 1989*

I cannot believe what just happened tonight. Last week Tara
basically told me that she has been making herself throw up. I've
been so upset by this that I haven't even been able to write. I made
her tell her dad, foolishly thinking he would scare her out of doing
this anymore. (It used to work when she was a child. She has always
been so frightened of his loud, booming voice.) Unfortunately, Lou
didn't exactly provide her with the scolding I was hoping for. He's
not even taking this seriously. He says this is a phase that she will

grow out of. This last week I've been hanging on to this, trying so hard to believe it, even though I know better. And now tonight has confirmed all my fears.

We ate dinner as a family, like we normally do on Sundays. After dinner Tara excused herself (after eating very little). I had this feeling in my gut. I walked down the hallway and stopped outside the bathroom door and heard her vomiting. I went back out to watch TV and Tara came out to watch with us. I didn't say anything to anyone. I was just sitting there in shock. I wasn't sure how to handle it or if what I thought I heard was real. Then I went to the bathroom before I said goodnight to her and I saw it. Right there in the bottom of the toilet were little pieces of vomit that hadn't flushed all the way. This is real now. I can't ignore it.

*Later—*

I'm not going to waste any time in getting her (us!) help. I can't sleep, again. Oh my god! I don't think I will ever forget. I knew it. I just knew it. Damn. I knew it! That damn kid is sick—really sick. Louie doesn't see how freaking scary this is. I don't know if I handled it right. I think I did. I hope I did! Oh god, oh god, oh god . . . grant me some wisdom. I really need wisdom!

*September 8, 1989*

I don't think I will ever forget yesterday's doctor's office. The office was nicely furnished, but not elaborate. I liked the plants in his office. Tara and I sat there listening to him behind his big desk tell us that Tara was indeed sick. This shouldn't have been surprising to me, but it was.

I came home and told Lou everything the doctor said and it was difficult for him to hear. The doctor confirmed her diagnosis of [anorexia and bulimia]. I could feel the anger in my body when he was talking. I was so tense, my stomach hurt. Wow, that is funny, huh . . . a tense stomach while finding out your daughter has an eating disorder! Ironic?? Part of me was watching and listening from outside myself, up in the corner of the room or something (disassociation?). I guess I was dissociating from myself because it was so difficult to be there, yet I knew I was doing the right thing by having her there. A part of me could not help being clinical, a therapist, yet I felt so incredibly stupid for being there! I know I selfishly wanted the doctor to see me as a fellow professional, yet I know he could not do that. He had to treat me, us, just like anyone else, because we are.

*September 23, 1989*

Things are busy, scary. I feel like I'm the only one trying to help Tara get better. Her father isn't helping at all. He just hides at work most of the time. Why is it that mothers are always left to clean up all the messes? Even the doctors and insurance companies aren't helping me. And God knows Tara is not helping herself get better. Why won't she just try? It's like she doesn't care whether she lives or dies.

# TARA'S DIARY

### 10/1/89

Mitch and I just had a huge fight. He promised me we would go out this weekend. I have been looking forward to it for weeks. He just called and canceled on me. He has a rugby party he's going to with the guys. I am constantly put second to his friends on his list of priorities. I feel like I'm going to explode. My heart feels like it's going to just break. I am so disappointed.

As soon as I got off the phone with him I ran to the bathroom and threw up. It's like I was doing it to hurt him in some way. I don't know how, he doesn't even know I do this. Every time I get angry at him I feel this incredible need to throw up, and when I do I feel a release from the anger. A sort of peacefulness comes over me. It takes away from the pain I'm feeling in my heart.

### 10/3/89

Yesterday went pretty good. I ate some M&M's in class and I couldn't wait to come home and throw them up, but I only threw up once today and once yesterday.

I really don't think I have a problem. Everybody keeps telling me that I do, and somewhere deep inside myself I feel like I should know the difference between right and wrong, but I feel like I can control it. If I really wanted to stop I would. I often wonder why I don't stop, but I can't come up with an answer. It's not as though I like doing it. In fact lately I've hated throwing up more and more. It seems to be getting grosser and less fulfilling. Lately I've been reading books and pamphlets on bulimia and anorexia to try and find out what is going on with me. I have to admit I see a lot of stuff bulimics and anorexics say that I relate to more than I'd like to.

### 10/6/89

Well today was another doctor visit with yet another specialist in Santa Barbara. It was pretty cool I didn't have to go to school at all today. And knowing how much I hate doctors, mom was compassionate.

I was pretty scared to go this morning, but he turned out to be nice. When I first got there, the nurses weighed me and took my height. I hate getting on scales. I am so embarrassed to have the nurses see what I weigh. When I went in to see the doctor, it was in an office not an examining room which was kinda nice—seemed less doctorish although I don't like the way he decorates, very boring and boyish. He asked me a whole bunch of personal stuff like if I was sexually active. At that moment I was so glad that I hadn't done the deed yet or I would have been so embarrassed.

After he asked all those questions, he took me in to be examined. He checked my throat and said it was burned and red. He checked my reflexes and said they were slow and sluggish. He checked my heart and said there was something wrong with it, but in the way he said it, it didn't sound too serious. He said my glands were swollen. All pretty much the same stuff as the other doctor. Then he called my mom into the room and told her I had [anorexia and bulimia]. He explained to my mom that this was the most serious kind of eating disorder because I wasn't allowing any sort of nutrients into my body. We know all this already! He said I had done an extreme amount of damage to my body in a short amount of time. I felt so proud when he said that. It means I'm good at what I do.

He said I had two options. I could either see a therapist and nutritionist for a while or I could enter a hospital and stay for one month and get treatment. I told him he was out of his mind if he thought I was going to go into one of those loony bins. I've heard of those places before and they scare me to death. I'll just die if my mom puts me in there. I'm really going to have to make sure I hide what I'm doing from her even more now. Which won't be too hard. She's never home anyway. Most of the time I'm in bed before she even gets home from work. She's fooling herself if she thinks she can beat me at this.

After I talked to the doctor I was told that I had to see a nutritionist for an hour. That lady was very nice and I actually enjoyed talking to her. She told me what foods I should start eating and that I wasn't getting enough protein in my diet. I kind of tuned her out because there's no way I'm going to eat the amount of food she was talking about. I will gain 400 pounds overnight if I do that. She said she is a specialist in this area and she promised me that the amount of food she was recommending would not make me gain weight. But I don't trust her. The only thing she said that really worried me is that if I don't get enough protein in my diet my body would start eating away at my muscles. I certainly don't want that to happen, but I don't want to get even more fat. So onward I go continuing my same habits.

### 10/10/89

I'm beginning to feel so weak. I can barely walk up the stairs at school anymore. I have to stop and rest half way up. I can't make them anymore. I feel like I'm going to faint sometimes and I'm not taking in enough air. And I don't have the high I used to get. I don't understand why. I feel sad when I think that I let this happen to me.

Who knows how I'll be able to handle my problems in the future. I don't seem to be doing a very good job of handling them now. I always had this picture of me in college, being successful and smart, having fun and being normal. Now I feel that's no longer possible. I can't focus on anything else but throwing up. And I'm starting to do it more. I used to only throw up about twice a day. Now I throw up at least 4 to 6 times a day. I can't help it. I feel like I really try not to throw up as much. Each day I wake up and say okay I'm only going to throw up twice today but then the day begins and I feel like I can't control it. The next thing I know I'm throwing up for the tenth time instead of the second. I feel helpless, like this goddamn thing has control of me and that's not the way it started. The whole point was that I had control, not the food and not anyone else in my life.

### 10/11/89

My mom's been really supportive and caring so far. I can see it in her eyes when she looks at me how worried and scared she is getting and I feel bad that I am making her so sad. My dad has really tried to be helpful, especially at the beginning. He tells me he loves me a lot more now but lately I see a change. He seems to be sick of wanting to help me. I can understand that this must get old after a while. My mom told my brother of my "problem" and I figured that he'd say I was just being stupid or something like that but he said to tell me that he loved me. It hurt me to hear that and I almost started crying when she told me. I don't think I've ever heard him say that to me.

I'm starting to feel scared about what's going to happen to me. I'm going to start writing even more because I think it helps me sort out my feelings. I need it to try and help myself understand what is happening to me and I want to keep this for later to remember this awful time in my life—like I would ever really want to. But if something should happen to me, I want people to know what I was thinking—that I didn't mean to make everybody so miserable. Or, if I do make it through this, maybe I'll actually show this to someone someday, who knows.

**10/12/89**

I forgot to write yesterday because I had a big Physiology test that I spent most of the night studying for. Monday was a day off of school so I went to see Mitch for a while but we got into a fight so I came home. I was telling my mom about it a little but then she had to go to work to help other people with their problems. Sometimes I wonder who's more important to her. I think that if it were a contest I would lose.

Jill came over for a little bit in the afternoon and we ate a pop tart and a bowl of cereal. As soon as Jill left I went into the bathroom and threw it all up. I couldn't handle the feeling of having food in my stomach, not when I was feeling so depressed about my fight with Mitch. But after I threw up I didn't know what else to do. I started to feel so depressed. All I could do was think about Mitch. I turned on our song and put the CD on repeat. I curled up in bed and listened to the song and cried for three hours. My eyes hurt today from crying so much. They're all puffy and red. My mom's calling me—we have to go to another doctor visit up in Santa Barbara. This time my mom and dad are going for a family session. This should be interesting.

### 10/12/89—later

That was simply not fun at all. We had to sit there and talk about how we felt about each other. My dad seemed mad afterwards, which I can understand. It's all my fault that we have to drive all the way up there. They both had to take off work, which is a huge sacrifice to them. My dietitian, Julie, said that I have to keep a journal of everything I eat now and if I throw up I have to write it down. I'm not sure if I'm going to actually tell the truth or not. I'll have to decide once I see how bad it looks.

### 10/13/89

I ate so much today and I only threw up once. I always seem to do that after a doctor visit. I feel like I owe it to everybody to keep most of what I eat down. I went out to dinner with my parents and I ate 3 tortillas, a slice of cantaloupe and 2 ice cream cones. It wasn't a binge because I still ate less than my parents did, but that was the most I've eaten in a long time.

Then tonight for dinner I ate 2 breadsticks and 6 bites of turkey. It was funny, after I ate I told my dad I was going to take a shower and he said, "wait" and looked at me funny. I said "dad I won't throw up, I promise," and he said, "okay, I trust you." I never really thought of throwing up until he said something, but if he hadn't said anything I definitely would have thrown up. I sat in that bathroom forever just looking at the toilet. It was like it was calling my name. I wanted so bad to get rid of what I had eaten, but I promised my dad and that meant something to me.

This Sunday, my family has to go to yet another psychologist for family therapy. What a pain this has all become. Sometimes I wish I would have kept my mouth shut and just killed myself with this thing!

## 10/14/89

Today is Saturday. Yesterday went okay, I guess. I've been eating more real meals lately and it's starting to scare me. I still haven't binged, but I feel out of control when I let myself eat at all. I hate eating. It makes it so difficult when I'm out with anyone. It seems like our whole social life revolves around food. It sounds funny, but people who don't know about my problem are constantly asking me, aren't you going to eat? and I tell them oh, I don't really eat and they look at me with this puzzled look on their face. I know it must sound bizarre to them but that's the truth. I just don't really eat anymore. Not unless I absolutely have to in order to keep from being totally yelled at. I end up just telling people that I have stomach problems so they'll leave me alone. It's not really a lie . . . I don't think.

I haven't been getting along with my parents lately. My dad seems mad at me for bringing all these issues out in the open. I'm almost scared to even write some of them down on paper, for if I do then that means that they really exist. Like the times when dad has hit Gregg and me, and mom. He doesn't realize the effect this had on us, well me I guess. Nobody else seems to even remember it. Am I the only one that feels the pain of his hands? Why doesn't anyone else talk about it? Gregg tries to deny that it ever happened.

I haven't had any serious depression episodes lately, but things still aren't any better. I'm supposed to be going out with Mitch tonight to see a movie. I'm really looking forward to it. I just hope he doesn't flake out on me. If he does then I will for sure go into a depression.

Mom told me the other day to just take each day one step at a time and see it as an accomplishment to finish that day. It seems like good advice, but that is a really hard thing for me to do. I want to see everything planned out years ahead. I think it's one of my biggest problems. I don't just live for today. I worry about next year and all the years after that.

Kyla and I have gotten even closer. I usually tell her the truth when she asks if I've thrown up. She's pretty good about not yelling at me too much. Jill and I are still best friends but I feel like this is moving us farther apart. I don't have anybody that can relate to the way I feel. I feel like I'm all alone here and like nobody else has ever felt this way. My friends don't really understand what I am going through. They mostly just try to lecture me about how I'm ruining my body. I don't understand how they can feel that way. They say they hate their bodies as much as I hate mine. So I just have the strength to do something about it.

**10/17/89**

I just found out that Colette [the daughter of my parents' best friends] is getting married. That really makes me think about my life. It really depresses me because I always thought my life was pretty good until I got caught up in all of this. I always thought I would grow up, find the man I love, get married, have kids and live, of course, happily ever after. Now I just hope I survive high school. I feel like all my plans are now just fantasies because I feel so bad about myself.

I'm getting to the point where I can barely function. I wake up in the morning and have to force myself to get out of bed. What I really want to do is sit in my room with the shade pulled all day long listening to sad songs. And I hate myself for eating. I don't know what's wrong with me, why I have to eat when I tell myself that I'm not going to. How will I ever stop throwing up if I can't stop eating? And I feel my love for Mitch has grown even more. I should be happy with my life, but instead I feel the way I do. I just don't understand how this could happen to me. I feel so abnormal and that's the hardest thing to feel at this age when being normal and fitting in is so important. And I hate keeping the stupid journal of what I eat for the nutritionist. It's a big fucking joke—like I'm really going to write down exactly what I eat and how my day goes, if I did it would look like this

Breakfast— ate a piece of toast and threw it up
Went to school ate ½ a candy bar . . . threw it up
Lunch— ate a bag of chips. . . . and threw it up
Was bored during 5th period, so went to the bathroom and threw up
Got home ate a bowl of cereal . . . and threw up
1 hr later—not sure if I got it all out so threw up again
Dinner—Ate 4 bites of chicken for dinner and pushed the rest of the food around on my plate so mom and dad wouldn't notice . . . then of course threw it up.

*When you write it down on paper it looks bad, which is why what I actually turn in looks something more like this*

Breakfast—bowl of cereal

Lunch—turkey sandwich

Dinner—1 chicken breast w/ mashed potatoes

**10/18/89**

*Last night I went with my family to see a new psychologist. It went okay. At one point I started to cry when we started talking about me going off to college and leaving my parents, especially my mom. I'm not quite sure why though. I never thought it bothered me, but I don't know why I reacted the way I did.*

*Yesterday was 4 months that Mitch and I have been dating. I didn't get to see him and I only talked to him on the phone for 15 minutes. That may be why I threw up so much yesterday (about 12 times). And today I threw up after school and about 30 minutes ago. They are beginning to turn into more binge-like episodes and it scares me, but not enough to stop I guess. I started my first class of jazzercise tonight. It went pretty good. I hope this will make it so I don't have to throw up anymore.*

**10/19/89**

*It's midnight right now and if my mom knew I was in the den typing she would kick my ass. But I had to talk about this. I just got off the phone with Mitch. We were talking for three hours. I finally told him about my "problem." He talked for a long time about how much it* bothered him. I instantly went over the deep end and told him I didn't want to see him anymore and to just leave me alone. He said he would never leave me alone over and over again. He said he would tell my parents how bad my problem was if I didn't listen to him. He said he wasn't going to give up on me and that I needed to understand what I was doing to myself.

I can't believe how I overreacted at the beginning of the conversation. All I heard was a small moment of frustration and my insecurities told me that he was going to give up on me. In order to protect myself from getting hurt I tried to push him away. I don't know how he sat there for three hours and took all that abuse from me and at the end of the conversation he could still tell me that he loves me. I really have to think about what he said tonight and I have to do something so that I don't lose the only thing in this world that means anything to me. I felt so sorry for myself tonight and he wouldn't accept that. I love him more now than I ever have. I guess I'm finally realizing that he really does love me and I could have such a good relationship with him if I resolve everything else in my life.

**10/20/89**

I just got off the phone with Mitch. We are having so many problems. I just can't trust that he loves me. Talking to him tonight, a scary thought came over me. When we were talking about breaking up, I thought of what I would do if I lost him and the word suicide was at the top of my list. I was seriously thinking about it. God I hope I make it through this year alive. I don't know if I will. I am so desperate right now; anything will set me off, especially if it's with Mitch.

## LINDA'S DIARY

*October 6, 1989*

It's 11:30 p.m. I have to remain calm. I am shaking inside, but I have to be calm. I cannot trust Tara. I know now I cannot even trust my own child to be honest with me. I can't believe getting help is so difficult. I feel like I'm the only one out on a small boat in a giant storm and trying to radio for some help, but all I get from shore are people saying it is sunny there so what's the problem? There is a problem, a BIG problem!

*October 16, 1989*

I cried at work today in our staff meeting (a little while ago). My associates were all very kind and let me just vent and scream a little. I feel so vulnerable. It is so very hard to maintain my work life knowing what is going on at home. It is like I have to have a giant wall inside my head. I know I must, I need to be ever so aware that all of this will negatively affect my ability to listen to others. That is why I let down with my colleagues. I told them to keep an eye on me, and give me honest feedback if I start getting too weird. I trust that they will be honest with me. I am worried that I will not be able to adequately maintain my "therapeutic distance." I know I will be able to. I just need to have more confidence in myself that I can handle all of this. I just have to trust the process. Breathe. Isn't that what I tell my clients? Practice the same stuff, Linda! Listen to yourself! Oh, God please help me!

*October 17, 1989*

I go to work with the feeling like my stomach is made out of lead. That is a funny thought for the mother of a girl with an eating disorder. Funny, hah! I don't know what she wants of me. Yes I do, I just can't give it to her. I feel pulled between trying to take care of her right now, trying to keep my business going, trying to pay enough attention to Louie. I'm doing a lousy job at all three. At least at work I have a persona to act out. I do try to be real, I really do. But I can't show all my personal pain because that is not what I am getting paid to do. I have to be there for my clients. I have to be there for my family. I feel like such a failure. Linda, you know that sort of talk will not help anything! I guess I just have to talk to myself sometimes to set myself straight. Focus.

*October 18, 1989*

It is late, again. What a surprise. This is getting to be a habit. It is good to be in therapy with the family. I feel a little calmer knowing we are going. The ride in the car is incredibly long, not because of the distance, but the tension that is in the car. We all know there will be things said, issues to deal with. The silence is deafening sometimes. At first I felt like I was dragging Louie along. I had such tremendous guilt, but I also knew I had to take a stand. It is hard for me to demand from him. He is so strong. I always have cowered in his presence. I can't in this case. I have to stay strong.

_October 22, 1989_

I want to believe that Tara is not throwing up anymore. She told me she did it just a few times. But then why does it seem so important to her? Linda, listen to yourself. You know better. Get a grip! This is an illness. She has an illness. It won't go away overnight. It is more serious than you could possibly imagine. Linda, you know about this stuff. Take a step back, breathe, focus, breathe. OK. OK. OK. Just focus on getting through tomorrow, one more day, one day at a time. That is so hard to do!

## LOOKING BACK

### TARA

I believe the first time I tried to vomit, I was simply experimenting with an unhealthy habit. Like sneaking a puff off my friend's cigarette or sipping the alcohol from my parents' liquor cabinet, my natural, experimental teenage rebellion was in full force. So I sometimes wonder why I didn't become an alcoholic or a drug addict. All I know for sure is that from the moment I hung my head over the toilet and felt the rush of adrenaline reach my temples, I knew I was in love. Like a heroine addict longing for the next hit, I would sit in class and daydream about when I would get the next opportunity to vomit. I craved the high it gave me, and I was obsessed with planning the ways I would elevate that high. My new obsession eased my anxiety and anger while keeping me thin. It seemed like the perfect coping mechanism.

Of course, it wasn't long before this "coping mechanism" began to take control of my life. In my weekly sessions with my psychologist, we worked on dealing with the emotions behind my disordered eating and finding alternative, healthy coping strategies. Yet despite this, I couldn't seem to truly get better. I began to wonder if I would even make it through my teen years. I was keenly aware of my mortality. I thought about dying almost every day. Dreading the idea of waking in the morning, I used to lie in bed and beg God to take me in the middle of the night. I stopped dreaming about the future because I was certain my future was bleak. I felt like I had ruined my life and there was no way to get it back on track. Ironically, this complacency may have helped ease some of the anxiety I was experiencing. I had become so depressed that I stopped caring about getting into college, maintaining a perfect persona, or pleasing my parents.

At this time, I went into a severe depression. I didn't leave my bed for 2 days. I didn't eat or drink anything. I got up only to go to the bathroom. I could see the look of disgust in my parents' eyes. I think they just thought I was being a lazy teenager. At my lowest point, I cut my wrists with a piece of glass from the picture frame that held Mitch's picture.

I was at a point that night where I didn't really want to die . . . I don't think. I simply wanted to feel physical pain. The pain I felt in my heart was too severe. I had to release it somehow, and throwing up was no longer enough. Cutting my wrists was yet another way to divert the focus away from feeling the real pain inside. Watching the blood rise to the surface of my skin gave me the high that throwing up used to give me. My parents walked in my room and saw me lying in my bed stoically staring at my wrists. I looked up at them with puffy, red eyes and said, "I'm ready, I'll go to the hospital."

Admitting that I needed help seemed like admitting utter failure. Yet I now realize that it actually took an enormous amount of courage to admit that I could not deal with my problems by my-self. And it took an equal amount of courage for my parents to accept and seek to understand my illness. Had my parents ignored my disorder (because of their own denial issues or otherwise), I am certain I would not be here today. In addition, had they not been so active in my recovery, I think the healing process would have taken much longer.

## LINDA

As I reflect upon the days that followed my eyes finally opening to Tara's illness, I remember first shock, then going completely into task mode. Once I "got it," I knew my husband and I had to act fast. I spent a lot of time on the telephone interviewing therapists and doctors. I knew Tara's behavior was serious. I had no idea at the time how serious it had already become, however.

When I asked Tara how many times she had forced herself to vomit, she said just a few. She lied. I wanted to believe her, but I knew even a few was too much. I knew from my limited training on eating disorders that this had to be treated, not ignored. I also knew that lying was a part of the illness, and I felt devastated to realize my own daughter would lie to me. I felt strong and weak at the same time. I felt strong in my conviction to get help; I felt weak and stupid for not acknowledging it sooner. The moment I discovered she cut herself with glass, I knew we would need to hospitalize her. I had no doubts then.

## CHAPTER 5, OCTOBER–NOVEMBER 1989
## THE HOSPITAL
*"Oh my god, what have I done."*

When I was first diagnosed with an eating disorder, the specialist proposed inpatient treatment. I adamantly refused to enter a hospital. I was afraid of hospitals, and it seemed like an overly drastic measure for a problem I believed I could control. But I got to a point where I could no longer function in my life. I didn't have the energy to go to school anymore, and I didn't believe I would survive if I stayed at home. Though at the time it felt like defeat, agreeing to enter the hospital was the most courageous thing I could have done. I had lost the battle to control my life on my own terms, and I now had to ask for help.

The hospital I was admitted to was in Santa Barbara, California. Blocks from the beach and surrounded by trees, it was an idyllic setting for any other circumstance.

Each day in the hospital was very structured and based on a set routine. The other patients and I would begin the day eating breakfast together in the cafeteria under the watchful eye of the militant nutritionist. While trying to overcome the first food hurdle of the day, we were tasked with planning our meals for the next. This was a colossal undertaking and took about an hour. Carefully completing the cafeteria form, we had to be sure we had chosen enough food to meet our required calories. Like a student apprehensively walking to the front of the class to hand in a paper to the teacher, we too made our dreaded journey to the front of the cafeteria for the nutritionists' approval. We were usually sent back three or four times before our food choices were approved. From breakfast we moved on to a series of group and individual therapy sessions. After lunch we often had time to explore our creative sides with art and writing sessions. Our favorite part of the day was exercise hour. We worked with a trainer to create an "appropriate" exercise schedule, which never fulfilled us. As we left the workout room, we would plot ways to burn more calories throughout the day. The schedule concluded with some education classes, where we were taught nutritional and mental health tips that would help prepare us for post-hospital life.

I found family therapy to be the hardest, yet the most helpful part of the recovery process. I was terrified every time I entered a family session, but by the time I walked out I felt like great progress had been made. This structured setting allowed me to express my feelings in a safe, controlled environment. I said things in therapy that I never would have had the courage to say elsewhere. During these sessions, my parents seemed surprisingly receptive to hearing my thoughts. They often looked stunned and wounded by what I was saying, but they were careful to appear calm.

## TARA'S DIARY

### 10/22/89

*I want this to take the place of the computer during my stay here. I didn't write on the computer for the last weekend because I could barely function. It started Friday afternoon when I told Mitch I thought it* would be a good idea if we didn't see each other. Finally he gave up—after days of trying to get me to talk to him and him saying how much he loved me—he finally gave up! I went into a big depression.

I went to bed at 5:00 Friday and wouldn't get out of bed. I just sat there and cried—Jill came up and tried to talk to me, but I pushed her away—she got really worried! My mom and dad were worried about me all night. Then at 10:00 PM I told my mom I was going for a walk and went to Jill's, got her bike, and went for a bike ride. It felt good to be up.

Saturday I got up and went out to breakfast then went to the gym with my dad then I came home and went straight to bed! (about 3:00 pm) I stayed in bed all night, I stopped eating and my mom and dad just kept bugging me to get up—they were really mad! Finally at 8:00 pm I went to Jill's—her parents were out of town—I went there to see people before I went into the hospital (I told my mom Friday I wanted to). Jill was buzzed and Kyla and Jill were with Ron and Tim so I didn't talk to them too much.

Sunday my mom dragged me out of bed—she was mad! I ate pound cake then threw it up—my mom knew it and got mad! I lay in bed all day and at 3:00 Dr. Sand called and we came to the hospital. When I first walked in, I was shocked. Dr. S said it was like a dorm room—this was a hospital for sick people—the nurses brought me to my room and tore apart my bags—they searched everything—that scared me. Randy [a part-time counselor] came in and he was nice—he helped, made things easier, but all I wanted to do was cry—and I did for the next 2 hours. Annie, Lorie and Justine are really nice and made me feel better. My parents left. That was hard—both knew I didn't want to stay. They watch me after I eat everytime—that's awful! There are chemical dependent people here too! It's 10:00 pm. I've been here 5 hours—things aren't as scary, but I don't want to be here. I miss my room, my bed, my friends, Mitch!!! Gregg called—a big surprise. He told me he loved me and that he was worried about me! We had the best talk we've ever had! I miss him.

### 10/22/89, 10:30 at night

Oh my god, what have I done. How could I have let my parents leave me here? This place is awful. It is a real hospital—cold floors, cold walls, cold beds. My parents admitted me about 3 hours ago. A nurse brought me to my room where she proceeded to open my suitcase and dump all my stuff out on the bed. She searched through everything. What the hell did she think I was gonna hide in here—food? She took away my razor. I asked her how I was gonna shave my legs and she said I could have a nurse supervise my showers or go hairy. What a bitch!!!

The ride up here today was so long and awkward. I felt the urge to apologize profusely to mom and dad. But, I wasn't sure where to start. Was I sorry for not eating, for throwing up, for cutting my wrists? Right now I'm just sorry to be alive. I feel like I have disappointed the 2 people that I have spent my whole life trying to please.

I want to snap out of it. I know nothing would please my parents more. But I just can't. I can't seem to drag myself from the depths of this shitty depression.

### 10/22/89, 11:00 pm

My mom told the counselor (a guy) that I hadn't eaten in days. So as soon as my parents left he brought me into the dining room and made me a turkey sandwich. I told him I didn't want to eat and begged him not to make me. He said that I had to. I asked him what would happen to me if I refused. He said they would eventually hook me up to an IV to get nourishment into me. In the end we compromised, he only made me eat ½.

I have to admit I have a lot more energy right now than I've had in a long time. And I didn't even throw it up!! But having this much food all of the sudden in my stomach is making me want to climb the walls. I can't just sit here feeling this full. I don't know what to do. I think I'll try to go talk to Randy. He seemed nice and compassionate. He said that the 1st night may be hard and I can go in and talk to him whenever I need to.

### 10/22/89, 11:30 pm

I just went and talked to Randy—he made me feel so much better—he's a neat guy he gave me hope—made me want to live!!!

### 10/22/89, Midnight

I just got done talking with Randy and I feel a lot better. He is reeeeally understanding. He is a recovering drug addict so he doesn't get the whole not wanting to eat thing. But he said he was an inpatient at this hospital a long time ago. And once he began to deal with his problems, he was much more equipped to handle life (I'm not quite sure what all that means, but maybe in here I'll find out).

### 7:30 am, 2nd day

I didn't write too much last night because I was too tired and I had a bad headache from crying. Yesterday at about 2:30 PM I started to really want to go home! I was sitting in a nutrition lecture and I started to get really bored so I related back to school and I thought about what Jill and Kyla and Mitch were doing at that moment and I got really upset. Then at lunch I didn't meet my 350 calories per meal so they made me drink the drink to make up for it. It was so degrading. What I really hate is PMM—Post Meal Monitoring. They make me sit in front of the nurse's station for a ½ hour—it's awful!

I called Kyla but she wasn't home. I talked to her mom and started to cry. I just miss everyone so much. Justine moved into my room yesterday. She's nice and I just try to follow her but she snores—bummer.

[Author's Note: Justine had just turned 40 and had been vacillating between anorexia and bulimia for 20 years. She was a strong woman who took me under her wing immediately. She didn't sugarcoat anything and helped scare me into recovery.]

Last night when my parents got here, I saw them and I started crying. I couldn't talk to them because I didn't want to cry. We went to family group and none of us said anything, but we came back to my room and had a long talk about how much I hate it here, but that I'll have to stick it out and be brave if I want to get better.

Yesterday when I got real down, I thought all I have to do is call Daddy and he would come get me. But I realize that I need help and that I'm getting it here. Me, Paula, Annie and Justine were in my room and I was wearing my sweatshirt that my bro gave me "Hot Buttered" some surf shirt and Paula (severe anorexic) looked at that and said, "Hot buttered, hmmm sounds fattening" we all laughed. I said only we would look at this shirt and say that!

I called Mitch last night. We had a really good conversation. We've had the best convo's since I've been in here. I miss him so much and I hope he's still there for me when I get out. He wants to come visit, but I don't want him to see me in here. I know I should just trust that he loves me and will no matter what, but with my self-esteem I have doubts—many! They just called us for breakfast . . . gotta go!

### 1:00 pm 2nd day

I just came back from lunch and Post Meal bullshit. I shouldn't say that, I guess I understand. Dad called me this morning. I was glad to hear from him and just to get a phone call.

My counselor is Christy. She seems nice. She reminds me of my mom a lot so I think it will be easy to talk to her. My psychiatrist is Dr. something. He's kind of a dork! Today is going better than yesterday, but every day is such a challenge to get through. I still hate it here. My hope is that I'll only have to stay one week. But like my dad always says, hope for the best, but expect the worst. I guess I'm getting a tutor in a couple of days. Sometimes I get so sick of talking about me and my feelings. There's only so much you can say in one day!

### 1:30, 2nd day

Well that sucked. Some gray old man just came in, dragged me out to some van and took chest x-rays. Yuck—be a little nicer—what an asshole.

### 3:10 PM, 2nd day Journal Class 10/24

We just had a "feelings" group and they pointed out to me that I am the youngest one here and must feel out of place—I do, I want to go home so bad. At about 2–5 PM I feel really lonely and sad—it's my worst time of day, night time is better because usually at home I'm alone at night, but here there's action and I'm with people. But then morning comes around again and I think I should be at school with my friends, but instead I'm in a lonely depressed hospital.

I miss my parents and my friends a lot. Every day I have to fight myself from picking up the phone and calling mom and dad and telling them that I can't stay here anymore. I was real depressed when I walked into my room and found 2 notes on the bed. One said my tutor's coming tomorrow—that makes me feel permanent—like I'll be here for a while. The second said my appointment with my family was next Monday. I guess I didn't expect to be here that long—awful feelings ran through me.

### 3rd day Wed. Self Assertiveness Group

| When I feel . . . | I need/want. . . . | I can. . . . |
| --- | --- | --- |
| Anger | Relief, Release | Swim, hit a pillow |
| Frustrated | Validation | Take a walk, talk to a friend |
| Boredom | Stimulation | Listen to music, exercise |
| Intimidated | Comfort, Safety | Take a bath, talk to people |
| Powerless | Hope, Control | Pray, meditate |

### 3rd day 12:30

It's after lunch. I ate a roast beef with mayo sandwich and I really want to throw it up. I told Justine and Annie and they're helping me.

But I'm afraid to go to the bathroom because when I see the toilet I'll want to.

### 4th day 8:30 Thursday

Last night at 12:00 the fire alarm went off in the hospital. It scared the shit out of me. Justine didn't even turn over. And it was right outside our room. I'm a lot more comfortable here now. I don't know if that's good or bad. I started drinking coffee here. Annie got me into it. There's nothing else to do here but drink something. It's almost like rebellion—all the regulations of eating and drinking.

### 4th day Thurs. 6:30 PM

Food for Recovery exercise

Calorie—evil, hate them

Means the unit of measurement of energy in food. Also means a lot make me fat—empty calories. Fatty—way of measuring amount of food fat fat fat!

Energy

Is something I get from food—a strength felt, gives power to body, strength to do exercise.

### 4th day Thurs. 9:45 PM

Quite a day. I'm sitting here hoping Mitch will call—not wanting to give in and call him. My credit card is probably up close to my hospital bill. My mom brought books and stuff this morning surprisingly. We saw each other for a min. I got kind of upset and started to miss her. She told me on the phone later that she went back to her office and cried.

In counseling with Christy today, a lot happened. I realized I felt I had to take care of my mom a lot. And Christy reminded me of my mom so I felt that way with her. That's so stupid to feel that way, but I do. I felt really mad and frustrated all day because I let someone (Christy) know how I really feel and because I feel fat. We went to the cafeteria for lunch today. Woo hoo—I saw all that food and before I knew it my tray was full, I didn't eat ½ of it but it scared me that I was that tempted.

I talked to Jill and Tim just now—they called. Jill told me she told Angie and Sara about where I was. That makes me kinda mad, but I know Jill wanted to tell them. I just wonder who else she told.

Annie got me started drinking coffee (decaf). I feel sick after I drink it sometimes though. I'm nauseous now. My food hasn't been sitting well and I know I've gained weight. I want to ask Dr. Sand how much I weigh and when I can go home. I just wish the asshole would come see me. I had a frustrating day cuz it's Thursday. I usually like Thursdays—I wonder how I'll ever make it through the weekend!

### 6th day Saturday

Last night (Friday night) Jill and Mitch came up to see me. I had a good time with them. I miss them so much. Mitch and I are doing really well. It was weird seeing them after I feel like I have changed this week. I was very nervous about them coming up.

Yesterday in therapy with Christy a lot came out. I have been angry all this time because my parents left me to go back to work. It's been really hard! I always feel like I'm betraying my family—Christy says I always talk like the text—I know too much I always say how I'm supposed to feel not how I really feel. I was pretty depressed this morning because it's the weekend and I'm stuck in the God damn hospital. But I feel a little better because shit-head Sand said I could probably go home on Friday—Thank God. I can't stay here any longer. I'll go crazy. Pam and Dave sent me flowers and balloons—that was nice. Jill, Dana, Kyla, Angie and Sara got me cards and stuff. That's nice too.

Annie's leaving Tuesday. It will be so sad without her. Justine wants to leave early also. I really don't want to be the last one here. Tom gave me a really nice card.

### 8th day Mon. 3:00 pm

I broke down in a session with Christy about dad and his yelling and hitting Gregg. We have family session tonight—I'm scared to talk about it. She told me to close my eyes and picture myself as a little girl. I pictured myself as 5 years old with long blonde hair, a straggly shirt and happy. She told me to bring this little girl with me all day and pretend she's there with me when I walk into the session. It really worked most of the day, but now she's starting to fade. I have to keep her here to fight for her in the session.

Last night Justine, Annie and I all put on the music and I taught them how to dance—it was great to dance again and we had a bonding. I saw Randy finally last night. But we never really talked. I'll miss him when I go.

I miss Mitch. I really need to talk to him and he hasn't called me cuz he's in Las Vegas. He said he'd call today and I know if he doesn't I'll be really upset. He doesn't realize that we have a lot to talk about, but

I don't think he wants to talk about it. I wish so much we could just enjoy each other like we used to. I think we'll be able to—I hope!

My visit with Gregg wasn't very good. He hasn't really changed. Just on the phone he sounds loving. I miss music, dancing, the ocean, love of friends (Jill, Mitch). Kyla I know is getting really wrapped up in Ron and just forgetting about her friends. I'm not going to be a caretaker and just let her deal with it. I'm afraid to go back to school and tell people stuff—natural I guess.

### 9th day Tues. 3:00 pm

Last night went really well with my parents. I told mom I felt abandoned and hurt when she went to work. And I told my dad that his screaming all those years scared me a lot. They took it well and said they knew I felt hurt with mom's work, but were surprised I was that affected by dad's yelling.

I called Mitch last night. I'm a bit worried about our relationship. He seems to only care about himself. I'll have to think about our relationship and see if it's helpful or painful to me. When I start to think like that I feel selfish, but I guess I need to be more with this disease. I've kind of decided to tell kids at school the truth when I go back. I'm a lot more scared than I thought I would be to go home. I'm afraid everything has changed or I'll go back and everything will be the same—the same routine—get depressed, purge to cope.

I know I have the desire to change but things can get so bad sometimes. I look back to the weekend I came here and how desperate I was with the glass out of Mitch's picture. I can't believe I wanted to die that bad. I hope I never get to that point again, or if I do I'll have *the strength (like this time) to tell my mom I need help. That's what saved my life.*

### 9th day Tues. 5:00 PM

*I just had a neat session with guided imagery. I pictured my beautiful place—grass, pond, nature. A butterfly came up and I asked it how I should live my life. He said to stop and enjoy all the beauty around me and to relax. It was enlightening. It was my inner self telling me—the wise voice inside me . . . Now I'm thinking whether I'll take that advice or not.*

### 10th day Tues. 9:30 PM

*I'm so pissed now. I don't know why I'm so emotional. It's Halloween—I just talked to my mom and bro—good conversations, but now I'm all alone on a night I want to be having fun. Jill said she would call—she didn't. She's probably with Tim. Mitch said he would call—he didn't—I'm sick of Mitch's excuses and lack of caring.*

*I feel anxious about getting parolled. What do I have to go back to? Homework, lost in school, problems with Mitch, with family and friends. How will I cope? Back to the same old thing—throwing up!!! I'm scared and angry. I feel sooo needy, but I really am. I need people right now and simple things like a missed phone call make me so upset and feeling like a failure. I went to Annie's room because she was feeling depressed and I cheered her up a little. Then Joel (her boyfriend) called and I just left. I totally understood, but that made me madder that Mitch didn't call!!!*

*"When I see you smile" by Bad English is on right now—that makes*

me think of Mitch. I was just sitting here feeling so inadequate because Mitch didn't call and I feel so lost because I didn't have any desire to throw up and I didn't know what to do. I felt like I had no place. I still feel that way. I'll have to do some sit ups or something to cope. I should be happy I cope differently, but I don't know what to do.

### 10th day Wed. Assertiveness Class

Maladaptive

(bingeing)

Preparing—I feel fat might as well eat—bored—uncomfortable/nervous, inadequate, failure, eat for avoidance—anger, destroying self cuz you're an asshole—pity

Adaptive

Food won't help—only make me fatter—emotional stuff (fat thought). What's goin on?? Alt. coping skills food short term solution. Food won't make it go away no black and white—manageable put on paper, when can get things done. Can't talk to that person, but talk to someone else who will listen. Permission to feel anger. DON'T PUNISH SELF

### 10th day Wed. 4:00 pm

I had a pretty intense day this morning. I was still mad because of Mitch and how insecure I am in our relationship. I want our relationship to live so badly. I talked to Dr. Teel about it cuz he knew I was mad. I really didn't know why until I started talking to him. Also I was sitting with Paula and Brandy—2 anorexics. They were talking about how fat they were and how much they weighed—that got me really depressed.

The two groups this afternoon were emotional for me cuz in both groups people said that I am so quiet and I never talk—they're right I'm too afraid of talking all the time or breaking down and crying. Good thing I'm leaving in 2 days so nobody can put me on the "hot seat." My bro and I talked last night. I was surprised it went so well— probably cuz he was ½ drunk—ha ha.

We actually talked about dad and his abuse on Gregg. I've never talked to him about that. I'm feeling such a bond between Justine, Annie and me. I'm really going to miss that when I go. It's funny when I first got here, I swore I would never miss a thing when I left—and I could hardly wait til that day, but now everything's different. I've made such good friends. I've learned so much and I feel secure here—normal I guess, but I still want to get out—but only to some things, like Mitch's love, Jill and Kyla's friendship, my parents' love, just the good things— impossible I know, but oh well!!!

### 11th day

I just came back in from sitting outside, I was looking up at the sky and letting the warm sun shine on my face—trying to get a little revitalized when again I heard Paula and Brandy talking about how fat they were. The 2 of them together barely break 100 pounds. 1 of them has a freakin IV hooked up to her arm just to keep her alive. If they think they are fat, oh my god, I must look like a whale!!!!

I feel so guilty that dad used to hit Gregg more than me—I've been thinking about that a lot lately. I don't know why dad wasn't equal about it. I guess because Gregg's a boy. There has always been a double standard in our house. I'm so mad at my mom for not stopping it. Why did she let dad hit Gregg like that???? Why did she hold me back when I used to try to get in between dad and Gregg. I'd rather get hit than have to watch him get hit and know there is nothing I could do to stop it.

### Last day Yeah!

Well the day is finally here. I'm leaving today. I packed my bags last night. My mom should be here in about an hour. I have butterflies in my stomach. I can't believe how nervous I am. I'm excited to get back to my own bed and to see all my friends again. But I'm going to miss Justine so much. She decided to stay here for another week.

Last night Christy came by my room to see me one last time. She took me into the bathroom and faced me towards the full-length mirror. She told me she wanted me to outline my body with my hands and to tell her what I saw. I did what she told me to and I told her that I saw a hugely fat girl that was disgusting. Apparently this was the wrong answer because she took me back to my room and went to consult the other "professionals." They almost weren't going to let me go home. I immediately changed my story, telling them that I really felt a lot better about my body since I've been in here—lie lie lie! Luckily they bought it.

## LINDA'S DIARY

*October 22, 1989, 11:00 PM, Hospital Day 1*

Well we did it. We actually committed our daughter to a mental hospital. I still have trouble even saying those words. I felt like I had no choice. I was afraid to leave her alone. I was afraid she would hurt herself. Even though we admitted her to the eating disorders unit, my main reason for putting her there is to deal with her deep depression. She's just turned into a zombie.

We didn't get there until early evening tonight. I spent all day on the phone with the damn insurance company. They have to make everything so difficult. What a pain trying to figure out our coverage and what this will cost. How can I think about money right now? I have to, though. I must have made 50 phone calls. But I was like a machine today. Pressing forward under extreme pressure. I just kept focusing on the crisis at hand.

The drive north felt so long. Very little was said by any of us during the hour ride. Lou drove. I sat in the passenger seat. Tara was curled up on the back seat. She made no eye contact. Her head hung low. We didn't know exactly where we were going. We had directions, sort of. When we found the hospital, we parked on a side street. It's Sunday evening, so there was little traffic. Things were very eerily quiet around the hospital. We got her bags, and all three of us walked through the large automatic main door entrance. We entered the spacious lobby. There was lots of seating on vinyl covered couches. Typical waiting room-type décor, but nice. Lots of large plants grew in giant pots that were placed all around. There was an odd stillness in the air.

There was nobody around to greet us. So we waited for an agonizingly long time. The volunteer ladies who usually man the reception desk had gone home. Lou walked nervously around looking for someone to direct us to the right area. He was making me nuts with his pacing. We were obviously lost. Tara just curled up on one of the couches. I walked quietly in circles.

Finally, Lou found someone to help. After several phone calls, and pages to several hospital workers, we were told we were at the wrong facility. This was the medical hospital. The psychiatric unit was a few blocks away. We got directions and left the building.

It was hard, no, excruciating, to step back into the car. I seriously doubted, at that moment, our decision to do this. I pondered our next move very carefully. Maybe we should just go home. Perhaps this was an omen, a message from God to turn around. Wouldn't it be easier to drive home and pretend none of this ever happened? Maybe Tara would come to her senses and realize just how serious this was! Maybe this is what she needed to know this was truly important. OK, now back to normal. All is forgiven. Let's just go home. We could even get home in time for some relaxing Sunday night television.

Damn. Again there was no response from her, not anything. The lump was real. This was not going to go away. I was hoping for one last reprieve. I was hoping she would perk up and say, "This has all been a joke, Mom and Dad. I really got you, didn't I?"

We started the car, made a left, then a quick right turn, down the block, to a much smaller building that was not easily identifiable. It was like having to go through it all again. Finding the first hospital, we thought was the right one, was hard enough. The walk through the barren Sunday evening streets was creepy enough. Having to get back into the car, again, was like someone saying you have not had enough pain, so now we'll pour alcohol over your open wound and make it sting even more!

It was a long, white stucco and brick building with a tile roof. We parked on the street, parallel to the front of the building entrance. The three of us walked slowly to the double door entrance.

The lobby was small, nothing like the spacious medical facility we had come from—serving as a bold reminder that this is a psychiatric facility. "You are in second class, not deserving of the fancy offices." There were a few brochures for reading about the program, groups offered, etc. We had to push a button and wait for what seemed like forever for a response. The door to the rest of the facility was obviously locked. The Sunday night's quiet had obviously fallen here too. We waited in silence. We waited not as a family. We waited as individuals hardly connected to one another at all. It was too scary to be connected. We weren't sure of our connections any longer. None of us was sure of anything, so we just waited.

At last, the door opened. We were escorted inside and this terrible, unforgettable day finally ended!

## Hospital Day 2

I am writing right now, but I can hardly feel my fingers. I don't want to write, but somehow feel I must. I don't think I will ever forget, but I don't want to remember either. Yesterday already seems like an eternity away. I can't believe how different things are now from just a few diary entries ago. How can things change so much in such a short time? Since Tara went into the hospital our lives have been turned upside-down. We are truly living through a crisis. And I use the term *living* loosely. We are more like robots on automatic pilot as we travel through our days, trying not to reveal that our family is falling apart.

I am really trying not to take all the responsibility and blame for all of this. But it is really difficult. I am her mother after all. I'm supposed to take care of her. How could I have let this happen to her? How could I not know she was in so much pain?

I am exhausted. My daughter is not with me. I have failed as a mom. No, I did the right thing. I really do know that. I failed her before yesterday, but I did do the right thing, the only thing, by having her go there. I know this. I just have to keep going. We are going to visit her tomorrow night.

I went to work today. I was okay. It felt safer having Tara in the hospital. I don't like it that it came to this, but I think this is what she, we, need. I can put aside some of my feelings during the day and just work. I have to go on and do what I do. This is going to be tough, but we will get through it.

*11:45 PM, Hospital Day 3*

We saw Tara tonight. She doesn't look like our kid. Seeing her there, among all those other people, those strangers, made her seem different. She is angry, doesn't want to talk to us much. She showed us around, her barren room with two sterile beds and the table where she puts the flowers sent to her from Aunts Karen and Nancy and Grandma. She showed us the other girls' rooms too. Many of them had small touches of a separate, personal life. Some had teddy bears or special blankets on their beds. Tara can't sleep without her "red blanket" she has had since she was a baby. Aunt Lois made that for her. Funny, here she is, far away from us, but still a little girl needing her baby blanket for comfort. All those girls seemed like very little girls. Many of them are much older than Tara is. I don't like it that she is there with older people.

When she was giving her dad and me "the tour," she seemed like she had settled in already, like she felt she belonged. I don't like that, but I do, I guess. The halls looked like hospital halls with a few boring pictures. It was weird to see a girl sitting outside the nurses' station like she was in time-out. All the bulimics are forced to sit there. Tara said she had to sit there for 30 minutes to let the food digest after having something to eat. She told us how much she hated that.

*10:00 AM, Hospital Day 4*

We had a family therapy night at the hospital. When I walked into the sterile overbearing room, I felt like two people. One part of me felt very comfortable in this setting. I was curious about how the group was going to be led. I was curious about the room décor, choice of colors, etc. This was the therapist part of me. This actually was a very small part, because the other, more frightened part took over very quickly. The mother part of me was concerned about how Louie was handling all of this. The mother part was hoping very much that our family would get something good out of such an uncomfortable situation. The mother part of me looked around at all the girls in the room and felt extremely sad. This part of me just wanted to hug them all and make it better. I felt guilty for even having the therapist part present. But I couldn't get rid of the dichotomous messages inside my head. I battled to extract the professional side of me and just be "the mom," but I couldn't, not totally. I couldn't help it, but I did know more than most of the other parents, at least about the illnesses present, and what the purpose of the group would be. Having this knowledge both helped and hindered me. I really had to work on just being present in the room once the group started. Actually, it was much easier once Tara came into the room (she wasn't there right away but came in with the other patients after the parents arrived). Once I saw her on the other side of the room it brought the Mom in me out right away.

Louie and I sat on one side of the large family circle that was comprised of bewildered parents and their complacent daughters. Tara sat far away from us. It was like we weren't even a family anymore. It almost felt like we were staging-up for a war with the line of parents on one side getting ready to do battle with the line of teenagers on the other. This is how it felt to me, but the girls did not look angry. Most of them just looked sad or like they were not even there, empty and far away. When one girl came into the room with an IV in her arm and looking like a prison camp resident, I knew this was all too real. I can't believe Lou stuck it out. I knew that he would have a hard time seeing someone so very ill. I know these intimately painful issues are hard for him to handle. I am glad he could stick it out. I was worried that he would get up and walk out when the heated discussions began, but he didn't. It hurt me, physically, to look at this girl with a barely there body. She couldn't have weighed more than 75 pounds.

I had a strange flashback to the past tonight as I sat there looking at this really anorexic girl. I am haunted by the memories of Loreen coming into our eleventh grade homeroom. She was wearing our blue plaid uniform skirt and a boring white short-sleeved blouse with a pocket over the left side of the chest. She was wearing the same uniform as the rest of us, but she did not look like the rest of us. Even under the "appropriate length" skirt she was beyond thin. The first thing I think I noticed was her pencil thin bones inching down beneath her skirt. These were supposed to be her legs. They really were just bones with a very thin covering of skin over them. Her knees were like giant round balls in relation to her bony legs. Her shoes looked oversized on her, like she was playing dress-up and wearing big-people shoes that didn't really fit. Her face was caved-in, and furry. I didn't know what this was about until I was in graduate school and began to learn about eating disorders. She probably was cute at some point, but at sixteen or seventeen none of us at school could see anything but some weird girl we didn't want to understand. We just knew she was different.

As it turned out, Loreen lived right around the corner from me. We carpooled to school every day. Her sister was a year younger and nice as I remember. It seems so strange now, but none of us ever asked Loreen why she was so thin or why she never ate. If Loreen was driving, we always stopped at the Thrifty Drug store on Mission Street in Oceanside. It was not really on our way home, but she always wanted to stop there after school. We would go into Thrifty's as a giggling bunch of Catholic schoolgirls and stand at the ice cream section in front of the store. They had lots of flavors to choose from as we peered through the glass panels to make our choices. Loreen's sister, our other classmate, who also rode with us, and I would always order a cone. I am embarrassed as I am writing this that I cannot remember their names. It bothers me that I can't remember Loreen's sister's name. Why is that? Oh well, anyway Loreen always ordered her ice cream in a cup, "to go." She never ate her ice cream in front of us. She always put her covered cup next to her just in front of the gearshift on the floor. It was always the same each time. We asked her about this once, I remember. She told us she just didn't like eating her ice cream until she got home. We accepted that! I can't believe it now, but we accepted this lame excuse. She never again talked about her eating habits, and we didn't ask. But we did ask her sister one day about Loreen's weight and her odd eating habits. She told us that one day in her freshman year, Loreen just stopped eating because a boy she was going with called her "fat."

As adolescent girls we talked among ourselves about how terrible she looked, and how "weird" she was in general. We were mean and unkind to her. I know we shunned her, didn't include her in our activities and mostly just avoided her. I know now we were avoiding ourselves, the uncomfortable feelings of being around her. I think we all knew, on some deep level, that there was something terribly wrong, but we felt helpless to do anything about it.

Loreen graduated with our small Catholic girls' school on June 8, 1968. We were all excited and happy that day. The day before, many of us, not including Loreen, went to one of our classmate's apartment by the beach. We had a uniform cutting party. We cut up all our blue plaid skirts and threw the pieces into the Pacific Ocean. We didn't worry about littering or the environment. We just wanted to be rid of high school. We also wanted to be rid of all the resentments and bad experiences of high school. I think that one of those blue plaid pieces of wool represented Loreen as well. I know I personally did not want to think about her bony image anymore.

In December of 1968 I heard a rumor that Loreen had gone up north, around San Francisco somewhere, to a hospital. She died not too long after. It was called anorexia. It was the first time I had ever heard of this. It was the first time anyone said she had a disease. I felt sad, and guilty for not recognizing her illness. How could I? The adults, her parents, the doctors, didn't know what was going on. It was not long after that there was more written about anorexia and eating disorders. It became something talked about on television. In 1968 no one knew about this. We just knew we couldn't talk about it and that it scared us. It still scares me.

At the class reunion that was held several years ago Loreen's sister was there. She didn't look much different than in high school. She had the same thick long brown hair. She confirmed the rumor that her sister had died of complications resulting from anorexia. I don't think I said anything much to her—another missed opportunity. As I write this here, today, I realize how I have carried Loreen with me all these years, and probably always will. I feel guilty for not knowing, not doing something. I was judgmental and self-righteous. I could have been more compassionate.

As I looked tonight at the girl with the IV in her arm I wondered if my own daughter might end up also tied to a feeding tube. Will Tara also look like this girl? Will Tara have fur on her face like Loreen? I cannot think that far ahead. I have to stop the pictures in my head or I will go crazy. Obsessing over her future hurts me in my bones, to my core. It seems as though time has been elongated. Just a few hours ago seems like an eternity. I am so terrified of the future that I have to force myself to be right here, right now. I cannot worry about whether Tara will end up like those other girls in the hospital.

We got through the family night. Lou and I didn't talk much on the way home. It was another long ride in the dark, late at night. We both had to get up early to go to work. I don't think we didn't talk because we didn't have much to say. I think we didn't talk because we had too much to say, but were so overwhelmed by what we had seen and heard at the hospital. It was so hard to leave Tara at the hospital. It seems so unnatural. She belongs with us. I know intellectually that if we keep her with us she might die. So, we drove home without her, in the dark.

I can't believe I typed so much. Glad to have the time today to do so. This seems to help, a little.

## 9:00 PM, *Hospital Day 4*

I went to work. Somehow I separated my personal life from the professional self. I find myself saying words to clients that I know I need to hear for myself. I am consulting with my colleagues. I really have to keep myself straight. I have to trust that Tara is learning what she needs to learn.

## 9:30 PM, *Hospital Day 5*

I drove an hour this morning just to see Tara briefly. I brought her the things she said she needed. I didn't want her to see how much all of this bothered me. She needs to be dealing with her own feelings, not be worrying about mine. When I got back to the office, I closed my door and just broke down in tears. I pulled myself together, though. I asked my associates not to say anything to me, or be too kind, because I have to be strong right now. I can break down later, not now. I just have to get through this, help my family to get through this. There will be time for falling apart later.

### 8 PM, Hospital Day 9

We had a family therapy session with Tara in the hospital. She said the necessary things to me. I knew she was feeling all these things, but it took her so long to get them out. It sure would have been easier if she had told me years ago. I would have listened . . . I hope I would have listened. If it took this long, then this is how long it had to take. I have to have faith that this is how all of this had to go.

I was so nervous when she started talking to her father. My first instinct was to defend him, to step in and stop her from talking. I knew I couldn't do this, but it is what I wanted to do. I was very proud of her for saying the words to him that I could not say. She had to say it. He wouldn't have listened to anyone else. I just sat back and bit my lip. It is hard for me to not jump in. It is hard to stop talking, even when I know better.

### 4:30 PM Hospital Day 10

It kills me inside to hear about how Tara has been self-destructing. And I don't understand any of it. The things she has said, my abandoning her by going to work, Louie's yelling, his temper . . . why Tara? Why this? Why so much? The therapist part of me understands too much . . . the parent, not enough. I remain confused, and very terrified!

### 10:00 PM, Hospital Day 10

Gregg and I spoke with Tara tonight. It was a fairly good conversation, although I can hear the pain in her voice. I feel so detached from her. It's so difficult not being able to see her everyday—just to know that she still exists. It's very difficult to just give her over to this hospital and trust that they will help her. I feel like such a failure as a parent. In spite of this, though, I have not gone back to self-hatred, a typical reaction of days long ago. This has surprised me, especially since there is a real reason to doubt my effectiveness at the one thing I tried to do so well—parent. I never thought I was faultless, rather I knew I didn't know a lot of things about parenting, so I had to try to learn even harder.

### Hospital Day 11

I am feeling very anxious about Tara's return home. I feel guilty for even saying that, but I can't help it. Things have been somewhat calm around here without her. Of course, she has rarely left my mind since she went into the hospital, but at least I know she is safe there. When she comes home I'll be constantly worrying about what she is eating, how she feels and what horrific things she is doing to her body.

## LOOKING BACK

### TARA

At the time I entered the hospital, my world was spinning out of control. I could no longer deny, even to myself, the hold my eating disorder had over my life.

The hospital experience was critical in breaking through my initial denial and creating a platform for long-term recovery. I was able to face painful issues while soothing the pain I had been harboring for so long. I learned a tremendous amount in a short period of time. My recovery was successful because I was committed to absorbing everything I could. I would fall into bed exhausted at night, totally drained from the day's work.

But no matter how long my hospital stay was, no amount of time would have prepared me for the harsh realities of after-hospital life.

### LINDA

As a mother, accepting and coping with Tara's eating disorder was a difficult process. The fact that I am also a family therapist added another layer of complexity. I kept working during this time, and I was careful to separate my personal family crisis from the pain in my clients. I did a lot of consulting with my trusted colleagues who luckily were honest with me when I needed it the most. Still, at times I felt like a fake, considering my clients often thought I had all the answers.

When I first truly realized that Tara had an eating disorder I knew, because of my training, what we were facing. I had to admit that this was not just about Tara; it was about our whole family. And I was utterly embarrassed and ashamed that I had missed this with my own loved ones.

Initially, Louie did not believe me when I told him Tara had a problem. I was scared to stand up to him and to remain firm that she—no, we—needed help. Amazingly, though, I discovered, in telling him, that I was able to believe in myself and the skills that my profession had taught me.

As Tara began inpatient treatment, I was scared about what family issues were likely to come up. I realized that problems like eating disorders often cover deeply hidden issues and feelings within the family. I had already had deep personal therapy to deal with many of my own childhood issues. I knew the pain, and the elation, of finally facing these. A bigger fear now was that my daughter—and my family—would also have to face such issues.

# CHAPTER 6, NOVEMBER–DECEMBER 1989
## BACK HOME
### *"After everything I've been through, why am I still doing this?"*

The day I left the hospital, my emotions were a mixture of excitement and apprehension. I sat quietly in my room, fearfully anticipating my mom's arrival. I felt guilty for causing such chaos in our family, and I knew the hospital stay must have cost a fortune. My mother arrived with a stoic, uneasy look about her. She was all business, signing the necessary papers and taking in the last minute tips. I stood next to her picking at my nails, anxious to leave. Arranging for my discharge seemed to take forever.

It was a warm, sunny day, and when I walked outside, I stood for a moment and let the sun hit my face. I felt like a prisoner being released from jail, tasting freedom for the first time. As Mom and I drove quietly down the bright, California coast, there was an overwhelming tension inside the car. The silence was broken when Mom asked if I wanted to stop and have lunch. I panicked. Just minutes out of the hospital, and I was faced with an uncomfortable food situation. I was afraid if I said, "No, I'm not hungry," she would turn the car around and take me back to the hospital, so I agreed to stop.

As I entered the restaurant, feelings of nausea began to take over. I ordered a "safe" meal, which consisted of a sandwich and fruit cup. After we finished eating, I got up to go to the bathroom. My mom's eyes bore into me. "Are you sure you want to do that?" she asked. I really did have to pee, but I said, "That's okay, I can hold it." I felt like if I walked into that bathroom, I would disappoint her even more than I already had.

The first few days home were difficult, to say the least. The loneliness of my former life came flooding back. Each meal was an obstacle ahead of me. Each meal I kept down was a triumph to be celebrated. I tried very hard not to vomit and only restrict if I really felt the urge. And although I was purging far less than before I entered the hospital, I couldn't get myself to completely give it up.

I started back at school immediately. The first day was horrible. Any questions I had about whether anyone knew where I was the last 2 weeks were quickly answered as I walked through the halls. The stares and whispers followed me all day. I felt like a freak. I was certain that I had just been tattooed with the word "crazy" on my forehead. But in the following days, some kids began to talk to me about my illness. I respected the ones who came right out and asked, showing their genuine interest and concern. I was open and honest with them, answering any questions they had. Somehow I felt lying to them would intensify the shame I was trying to escape. Before long, I became the poster child for eating disorders, and suddenly girls I didn't even know were confiding in me about their own poor body image and eating issues. I was shocked to discover that so many others experienced the same feelings I did. It was at this time that I realized there wasn't enough open communication about this subject, and I became determined to do whatever I could to help change that.

# TARA'S DIARY

*11/10/89*

Well, I've been home for a week now. And just as I feared, things suck! It's like I've forgotten everything I learned in the hospital. I haven't even written in my journal all week, probably because I haven't wanted to face the reality of my post-hospital life.

At first I was excited to be home. I missed everyone and everything so much. I'm so happy I get to lie on my own bed again. Yet, when I do, I'm reminded of the days before I went into the hospital, the terrible things I did. I look at the picture of Mitch in the frame sitting on my nightstand, something that should make me happy. But now it reminds me of how desperate I was just weeks ago. And it only took a day and a half for me to start throwing up again. I don't know what the hell is wrong with me. After everything I've been through, why am I still doing this? My parents have spent thousands of dollars to help me stop throwing up and I'm wasting all of it. Mom and Dad would absolutely die if they knew I'm doing it again.

Life is just so hard right now. Going back to school was terrible. As I walk through the halls I can feel the hundreds of eyes on me, all wondering how I can be so screwed up. I'm already so sick of their pitiful glares. How the hell am I going to survive the rest of high school like this? And the fucking teachers are even worse. I had to stay after school to talk with Mr. Hogan about the 2 tons of work I have to make up. I was standing next to his desk as he explained the assignments. Then out of the blue he says, "Tara, I don't understand why you're doing this to yourself. You're not fat."

He then takes out a Snickers bar from his desk drawer and hands it to me. I politely decline it and he forces it into my hand. I try to give it back and he starts to get angry. He insists I eat the candy bar. I said, "Okay, I'll eat it later."

"Oh no," he says. "You're not leaving this classroom until I see you eat a bite of the candy." I couldn't believe what I was hearing. I was totally in shock. But I unwrapped the candy and took a small bite. I strategically placed it in the back corner of my mouth and left it there until he was done explaining the rest of the homework. Then I walked out of his room and spit the runny brown mess over the school railing. There was no way in hell I was going to eat even one bite of a candy bar. I'd rather die then allow all that gross chocolate to melt into fat on my body.

**11/24/89**

Oh my god, Thanksgiving was sooo hard this year. Talk about an excruciating day. I obsessed all day about how I was going to handle all that food on the table—all my favorite foods. I always overeat on Thanksgiving—that's what you're supposed to do. But I can't handle the feeling of food in my stomach yet. I knew if I ate too much I would throw up for sure. And my freakin' parents—god talk about uncomfortable. I felt like they were watching me all day long. Mom was trying to be really considerate and helpful, but I think they made it worse by being so focused on "it."

I ended up just eating a normal portion—which was totally unsatisfying—took all the fun out of the holiday and all. I didn't throw up yesterday, but I have been wanting to bad all day today. I don't know why I guess it's just knowing I ate on Thanksgiving and kept it down. I'm just imagining how the food is sticking to my thighs and stomach right now as I type. I hate this! Why can't I just be normal? Eating is supposed to be just this thing you do to keep alive. Why has it become such an abnormal thing for me. Why do I think about it so much? Are other people like this? Am I focusing on eating/not eating in order to not focus on other things. What are those other things???? I need answers!!

**11/25/89**

Mom has been really good about trying to be supportive. I can see her really attempting to help me conquer this damn disease. Of course I'd never tell her this, but it means so much to me that she is trying to understand what I am going through and why I became sick. She's made it clear to me that if there is ever a time after dinner that I have the urge to throw up that all I have to do is ask her to go for a walk and that will be our code for "I'm in trouble, distract me." And lately I've needed her help a lot. We've been going on a lot of walks, which is nice because we also get a chance to talk on these walks. They are very soothing. It's like she's finally responding to the fact that I need her.

**12/27/89**

Mitch and I made plans to see each other on New Year's Eve. I'm so excited. I miss him so much—he's up at his parents' house in Paso and I haven't seen him for like 2 weeks. I'm going to go buy a new outfit to wear. We're going to hang out at Jill's cuz her parents are out of town. It's going to be so fun. Gotta go shop!

## LINDA'S DIARY

*November 9, 1989*

I can't believe how different things are now from the last entry in here. Tara revealed her eating disorder, went in the hospital—mostly (all) due to depression, which scared all of us, and tomorrow will have been home 1 week. I have come to doubt just about everything in my life, especially my parenting.

I am sitting here in bed reading *Through Divided Minds* (about Multiple Personality Disorder), and can't help (not the first time) but wonder what awful things might have—and statistically do in many cases—caused this in our family. In spite of this I have not yet gone back to self-hatred and some of my more typical reactions of days long ago. That rather surprises me, especially since there is real reason to doubt my effectiveness at the one thing I tried to do so well—parent. I never thought I was faultless—rather, knew I didn't know, so had to try, learn harder.

Almost every night now Tara goes into some kind of depression. It kills me inside to watch her self-destruct—and God I don't know why—oh the things she's said—my abandoning her by working—Louie's yelling, temper, etc.—but why her, so much?? The therapist part understands too much—the parent not enough—I remain confused, and very, very terrified.

I got a migraine Sat.—resulting in a trip to Urgent Care—1st need for Demerol shot in 6½ years. This isn't bothering me much is it! I am really not trying to take all the responsibility and blame and I don't feel bad about myself (weird?)—I have felt tremendous anxiety and tension. I'm trying not to enable—Jesus that is hard when it's your child who's suffering. I'm so afraid—I don't even want to say it—I won't—I fear bad things. Please let her, us, be OK.

*November 19, 1989*

I watch every move she makes. I try not to, but I do. I want things to be "normal," but I know they cannot, will not be. Tara seems happy, sometimes. She then, suddenly, will revert back to her morose, depressed self. I get my hopes up for a good day, and then they get dashed in a second. I know this will not go away overnight. I listen at the door of the bathroom every time she goes in there. I listen. I feel guilty for listening. The bathroom is such a private domain, but I can't let it be private for her right now. Maybe I am wrong. I have told her how uptight I feel. I have told her I am listening. We are doing a dance here and neither of us knows the steps. There is a lot of stepping on toes right now. And it hurts! Except in those rare moments when we do get into rhythm. Then it is good. Then we can hear the music the same way and it feels like eventually we will get the dance steps down right. I pray for that day!

*December 5, 1989*

Tara is in the den writing on the computer—probably about how awful I am. I'm trying really hard to be a "normal parent" and be mean and just let her get angry—they said to expect that at the hospital—for her to become a normal teenager. This is awful though. YUCK! Louie is out of town again—lots and lots lately. Of course as usual I get the anger, the acting out. Tara came home at 9:10 tonight. I told her she had to stay home Friday. Oh joy . . . I don't know if I will stick with it because I usually give 10 min. leeway—I figure I'll just let her be mad at me—this sucks.

## LOOKING BACK

### TARA

I walked out of the hospital physically and emotionally drained from the intensive treatment, but I was certain the worst was over. I knew I still had work to do, but I assumed that because I had served my time, I was well on my way to being cured. I met my new "old life" with a mixture of anticipation and dread. Reintegrating myself into my former life was much harder than I anticipated. It was like having to learn to walk and talk all over again. I had to change the way I coped with everyday issues. My first instinct was to throw up, and I would physically feel nauseous. I had to actively refuse that pull to my old ways. The life I knew before was taken away. I was stripped of my coping mechanism and expected to flourish despite that. I had to retrain my mind to handle life's daily problems in a completely different way, a much harder way. I now had to cope with problems instead of stuffing them down or throwing them up, and I had no idea how hard that was going to be.

My parents' participation in my recovery was one of the most important elements in my healing. When my mom was around, she had this maternal instinct that seemed to alert her when I was struggling with old habits. As I discuss within my diary, we developed a code. My mom would ask, "Do you want to go for a walk?" This meant, "You look like you want to throw up; let's get you out of the house." We'd walk through the neighborhood, breathing the fresh air and talking about nothing. By the time we returned home, my desire to purge was usually gone. I'm not sure I ever told my mom how much this supportive gesture meant to me. More than just preventing me from throwing up, it proved she was there to support me when times got rough.

My dad went out of his way to make sure I knew he loved me. He started hugging me more and wouldn't let me go to bed without telling me he loved me. He also created an environment where I felt like I could tell him anything. He made it very clear that he was always there to listen to me. It was almost like getting sick was a test I created to see if my dad would get scared away by my bizarre behavior. But he didn't. Quite the contrary, he made it a priority to know what was happening in my life and support me through it. I believe it was at this time that I first began to accept that my dad loved me unconditionally. That feeling of unconditional love was crucial to my ability to begin to love myself.

In addition to my parents' support, I continued to get professional help. Twice a week, I met with the psychologist with whom I had been working prior to entering the hospital. Plus, the family was supposed to commit to weekly family therapy sessions. I was also encouraged to attend hospital group sessions as an outpatient to ease the transition between the hospital and home. I viewed individual therapy as my much-needed support. I was even more committed to attending twice a week and often wished the appointments were more frequent.

Sometimes when I was having a bad week, I would ask my mom if I could skip school and drive up to Santa Barbara to attend a group session at the hospital. I thought she was so cool for saying yes. She recognized my struggles and allowed me to deal with them the way I saw fit. It showed that she trusted me and believed in me. The hour drive up the coast was a soothing, introspective treat. I felt like I was taking care of myself on these trips. After the group session I would take a walk on the beach and marvel at the vast ocean before me. Somehow the immensity of the sea put my problems into perspective. It was here that I was able to gain some objective distance from my life. To this day, the beach is the place I return to when life seems overwhelming. It continues to soothe my soul in times of trouble.

Family therapy, on the other hand, was hell, which was probably due to the fact that it was the most painful and revealing aspect of recovery. My parents seemed to feel the same. We went to the first few sessions and then never went back. Everyone seemed to get too busy and preoccupied with the trials of life. In hindsight, this was not a good move for our family. The few sessions we had in the hospital did not resolve the deeply embedded issues we held.

## LINDA

It still hurts so much to read what my own daughter went through. The small things she hated me for are part of adolescence, and I can accept that now. But recognizing that she felt truly abandoned by me, her mother, is almost more than I can bear. I never meant for any of this to happen. I didn't know how to correct the things that were wrong. I didn't know how to stand up for myself until I had no choice but to stand up for Tara. I didn't listen or act for a long time, but eventually I had to speak for her when she could no longer speak for herself.

At the time, I felt like we were the worst family and I was the worst mother, wife, and human being. I also consciously knew this crisis was necessary in order to bring things out in the open. Tara's depression and eating disorder forced the underlying unspoken issues in our family to the surface.

## CHAPTER 7, 1990–APRIL 1991
## PREPARING FOR AND SURVIVING SENIOR YEAR
### *"I want to be normal."*

At the time I wrote the following diary entries, I was busy filling out college applications. I was still filled with anxiety and doubt, but less so than I had been at the same time the year before. I was undecided about where I wanted to attend school, so I applied to several schools, giving myself more options. From San Francisco to San Diego, it seemed like I covered every school along the coast of California. The only thing each school had in common was being located close to the ocean. To me, the beach represented comfort, clarity, and hope, and I wanted to maintain that connection to the healing process.

Gregg was still in college at San Diego State University. He was enjoying school, spending more time surfing than studying. He came home to visit every so often, but always seemed eager to get back to school. He had started a new life, a life separate from our family unit. It was eventually something we all got used to.

On New Year's Eve, I made a vow to stop purging. Unfortunately, without this outlet, I was left to actually feel the pain. Just days after New Year's, the pain became overwhelming. Mitch and I broke up . . . again. This perceived abandonment sent me to new depths of depression. I once again removed the glass from Mitch's picture frame and cut my wrists, even deeper this time. It's hard to explain how this seemingly insane act could serve as a coping mechanism. Inflicting pain on my wrists took some of the hurt out of my heart.

That spring, Mitch graduated from college. I attended his graduation and met his parents for the first time. His transition out of college was a turning point in our relationship. He was now entering the "real world" and taking on new responsibilities. He got an apartment with a few friends and began the search for his career. This transition frightened me. I was even more afraid he was going to grow out of me. I was still finishing high school and he was living an adult life. We were at very different stages in our lives. The only thing we had in common was our love for each other. As much as we tried to prevent it, our different worlds continued to pull us apart.

My parents and I were trying to live cohesively together. We continued to irritate each other at times, but stayed committed to our Monday dinners, which helped to retain some sanity. My dad initiated Monday dinners at restaurants as an opportunity for the three of us to connect. It was difficult taking time out of our lives to discuss feelings and truly hear each other. But somehow sitting at a restaurant allowed us to escape our normal environment and connect on a different level. It was an opportunity for my dad to hear how I was doing and a safe forum for me to express concerns that had cropped up throughout the week. These Monday dinners replaced family therapy for us. Without them, I don't think our communication would be as productive as it is today. We had to learn how to talk to each other, and more important, how to truly hear one another.

I began to depend on my journal a little less this year. I wrote in it only when I felt I needed to. I didn't record a lot of the happy times in my life because I didn't need to. I basically used the diary as a place to dump all my negative feelings.

## TARA'S DIARY

### 1/1/90—New Year's Day

This is it. I'm making a fresh start to the new year. It's now the 90s and I don't want to be sick in the 90s. My New Year's resolution is to stop throwing up. I have made the decision that throwing up was the 80s and I'm not including it in my 90s plans. But, naturally, I left the 80s with a bang.

Last night Mitch was supposed to come with me to Jill's New Year's Eve party (her parents are out of town). He came over for like 10 minutes then just decided he had to go. The college dorms aren't open during winter break so he was supposed to stay at Jill's. He made up some lame excuse about staying at his buddy Tom's house. He left at like 8:30. He said he didn't want to wake Tom up by getting to his house too late. I just know something is going on. He's not telling me the truth. I can feel it in my bones. I was absolutely crushed. I had been planning for this night for weeks. I got a new outfit. I painted my nails. I haven't been eating too much, and all for nothing. He better not be screwing around on me or I'll just die.

After he left I was so depressed. Jill got out the tequila and I think I did about 20 shots. Okay, not that many, but a lot. I felt so angry I didn't know what to do. I couldn't focus on anything else. I've been trying so hard not to throw up, but I felt I deserved it last night. Besides the fact that it felt like the tequila was burning a hole in my stomach, I had to somehow release the anger I was feeling. But as I was hanging my head over Jill's toilet at 11:52 PM, I made a vow to myself. I promised that this would be the last time I made myself throw up. I'm really going to try to find another way to cope with my feelings. It was like I left my body and looked down at myself from above. I saw myself alone, pathetically hurting my body when I should have been out partying with everyone else. I decided I don't want to live like that. I'm turning a corner in my life. God please give me the strength to uphold this promise.

### 1/6/90

I'm sitting on my bed here no better than I was 6 months ago. All the time I've spent trying to get better and yet I still just want to die!!! Why am I so screwed up? Why can't I just go away? I don't want to cause my parents pain. I don't want anyone to have a funeral for me. I just want to disappear. Why can't God just ease my pain and let me go. I want out of this life. I can't be here anymore.

I tried—I tried sooo hard to make myself into the person everyone wanted, and I have even stopped throwing up. But I can't do it anymore. This stupid picture frame is just sitting here calling my name. I've tried to ignore it, but it still has the same jagged edge I cut my wrists with before. I'm trying to put off doing what I know I'll end up doing by writing in this stupid journal. I don't know what I'm looking for—It's not like I'm going to become instantly enlightened and find all this joy in my life. But I'm not going to kill myself either. I swear. I don't even have the courage to do that! I just want to cut myself a little. I have to feel some other pain than what is in my heart right now!!! My mom said I couldn't have been trying to kill myself last time because I cut my wrists horizontally instead of vertically to coincide with the veins. Well shit I didn't know the "correct" way to kill myself. But now that you've taught me, mom, I'll show you vertical cuts you BITCH!!!

**1/14/90**

Mom and dad actually invited Mitch over for dinner. I can't believe it. They really are trying to help me. I'm so happy they are finally seeing how important he is to me. It means so much to me that they are trying to put their feelings aside and give him a chance.

**1/21/90**

We have all these stupid new rules in our house—mostly about eating. They always talk about how I developed an eating disorder as a way to gain control of my life and now they're trying to control everything I eat. I don't understand how that is going to help me recover. Obviously I hate the fact that I have no control in my life—this is only making it worse. I have to write down everything I eat and then add up the total calories. And they bought Ensure for me to drink on the days I don't meet my calories. What is such a joke is that they are still never home and wouldn't have a clue how many calories I actually took in. And it's not like I'm going to try to not meet my daily calories, but I'm just saying if I didn't want to try to get better, it would be a piece of cake to fool them.

**1/25/90**

Why am I struggling so much? Why? Why? I want to be normal. I don't know why I can't just make myself happy. I'm so tired of feeling sad. I'm going to my stupid therapy. I haven't been throwing up. So why am I not better? I have worked so hard this month to stick to my promise to not throw up. It has been so freaking hard. Nobody has any idea how much I struggle with it every minute of every day. Mom thinks it may be hard for me just around meal times. She doesn't realize that I obsess over not throwing up just as much as I used to obsess over planning to throw up. I still sit in class all day and develop "plans" to keep myself out of tempting situations.

### 2/5/90

I hate him! Why do I put up with this shit? He says he's going to call and he doesn't. Then when he does he gets mad that I'm upset about it. He's such an insensitive jerk! The sad thing is I think most men are like this. They are so inconsiderate. He just can't understand why I'm so sensitive about a phone call. It's not the phone call—it's what the phone call represents. When he ignores me like this it shows me that he could give a shit about me. He couldn't possibly love me if he treats me this way. I should just break up with him again. I'm going to. I'm gonna write him a letter and mail it to him. I never want to talk to him again. But I still love him so much. It's going to hurt to be without him, but that's the only choice I have.

### 2/10/90

Mitch and I went out tonight. We had a great time. Things are much better since our break up. I know it wasn't a long break up, but I think it did us both some good. I think the letter helped him understand how I feel and he really didn't want to not see me anymore. He told me how much he loves me and wants me in his life. I really needed to hear that I guess. Hopefully things will be smooth sailing from here.

### 3/11/90

I had a really terrible morning with my mom today. I slept through my alarm this morning so was obviously running late. I raced around the house throwing on clothes and brushing my hair. I walk out to the kitchen (to go through the garage door to leave) and my mom blocks the door. She said, "You're not leaving without eating breakfast, you know the rules." I told her I was late and I'd grab a snack at school. She said, "I'm sorry but this is not negotiable."

I haven't been that mad in a long time. I was not trying to restrict. I simply was trying to get to friggin school on time. Is there some crime in that? She quickly threw a piece of bread into the toaster. I stood there glaring at her as it toasted. When it popped up I grabbed it and started to head out the door. She again blocked the door and said, "You have to eat it here so I can see you." I was in absolute shock. I cannot believe she is trying to be this controlling. So I stuffed the entire piece of toast into my mouth and pushed past her out the door. She stood in the doorway watching me walk to Jill's car. I'm not really sure what came over me, but when I reached the end of the garage, which I deemed a safe distance, I spit all the bread out on to the garage floor and I stared right into my mom's eyes as I did it. Then I just turned around and got in Jill's car. She didn't even say anything. I think she was in shock.

When I came home from school the bread was cleaned up. I feel kinda bad about it now. I know it was really disrespectful, but I had all this rage inside me and I didn't know what to do with it. I'm tired of stuffing all my feelings. From now on when I'm angry I'm going to show it. And if they don't like it then that's just tough. They are the ones paying for me to go to these wacky psychologists giving me even wackier advice. If they don't like how I am turning out then they should stop making me go.

**4/14/90**

Aunt Nancy (Dad's sister) is out visiting with us. I love her, she is so much fun. She is so full of energy and life. I wish I could be more like her—carefree and happy. Mom and I took her to Palm Springs for the weekend. We had so much fun! It was the first time in a long time that I felt "normal."

We went to this huge water park. We were all laying out by the wave pool all day. And whenever I would get up to go cool off in the wave pool this one really cute lifeguard would stare at me. Finally one of the times he walked over and started talking to me. And he asked me out for that night!! Unfortunately we were leaving at the end of the day. I was so bummed cuz he was such a babe. Even though I didn't get a chance to go out with him, it made me feel so good. I can't remember a time when I've felt so comfortable in my skin. I was wearing my blue and purple bikini and I'm really tan right now so it looked pretty good on me. I was actually up and walking around in just my bikini. I was a little self-conscious of course, but not nearly as bad as I have been in the past.

After we left the water park we drove to the strip to eat dinner before we headed back towards LA. It was so nice sitting outside under the water misters eating and talking. I was in heaven . . . until of course I got up to go to the bathroom and my mom grabbed my hand and said, "Are you okay?" I was so shocked that she said that. I wasn't even thinking about going and throwing up. I was having the best day ever and she just completely ruined it. It's like I had finally forgotten about how screwed up I was, but leave it to mom to go and remind me. All I wanted was one day to not be sick, not be depressed, not have an "eating disorder." I pulled my arm away from her and said, "I'm FINE mom."

I was depressed the whole ride home. I didn't want to go back to the crap at home. I was laying my head against the car window fantasizing about staying in the warmth of the desert. I love the sun. It gives me energy. It lifts my spirits. I don't think I could ever live where it is cold. If I lived in Seattle I think I would have killed myself years ago—if I stay in California I may actually see 30!

### 4/22/90

Yesterday Kyla, Nicki and I drove out to Palm Springs for the day. We had so much fun! We cruised the strip and saw so many cute boys. I was happy that my parents listened to me and let me stay out later, but I was very nervous about getting home on time. They said I had to be home at 1:30, so I made us leave Palm Springs at 10, giving us plenty of time to get home. It usually only takes about 2½ hours to make it. My friends were annoyed with me, but I didn't care. But then on the way home workers were doing construction on the freeway. Who does construction at midnight in LA? We were stuck in traffic for 45 minutes, then we sped so fast to try to get home. They dropped me off in front of the house and I ran down the driveway to get in the door in time and I fell and scraped up my whole right leg. I was dripping blood as I stumbled into the house at 1:25 (whew, five minutes to spare). And my parents weren't even waiting up for me! They'll never know what I went through just to respect them and make their curfew.

### 6/2/90

Things are going well. I'm lifeguarding and teaching swimming again. I'm happy to be back with the kids. It's like they give me energy and lift my spirits. The sun also makes such a difference. I can't believe what I've been through since last summer. It's like this year has just been one big dark cloud. I'm so happy to see it clearing.

**6/9/90**

We still do our Monday dinners. They have been going pretty well. I'm actually feeling like I'm getting a lot closer to mom and dad. Things with Mitch are going okay. Ever since he graduated he's been really weird. I know he's stressed about finding a job, but he's been really taking it out on me. I'm so afraid he will get a job far away and then he will leave me. I don't know what I will do if that happens.

**6/12/90**

There is this one little girl at work who is so damn cute. She is in the kindergarten group and has bright blonde hair. She is such a good little swimmer—I love teaching her and seeing her get so much better. She makes me want to have kids. I think I would be a pretty good mother. I feel like I have so much love to give. I'll probably never have the chance.

**6/20/90**

Mitch got offered a job in Lubbock, Texas. He doesn't know what he is going to do yet. I have spent the last 2 days since he told me pretty much in hysterics—I mean I'm still working and everything but every spare second I have I'm crying. He said maybe I could go to college out in Texas. But that's still a year away—we will never be able to be apart for a year.

**10/2/90**

God it's been so long since I've written in here. I've just been so busy. My classes are really easy this year. Things with Mitch have been good. I really think he might be the one for me. I don't want to date any of the guys at school. All I want to do is be with him. I just wish he was more attentive to me and wanted to be with me more. He always wants to hang out with his friends. I mean I want to hang with my friends too, but I have this really intense urge to see him and he doesn't have the same for me. Maybe I should break up with him. I'm sure I should. But I don't know if I'm strong enough to be on my own. Everytime I try to be apart from him he calls and I just end up getting back together.

**11/8/90**

I love being a senior. I didn't think it would make that much difference, but I love being the oldest at school. I have joined ASG [Associated Student Government]—it's really fun. I like being involved in planning rallies and stuff. We always know more about what's going on at school than anyone else. It's pretty cool.

I've been thinking that I should date guys from my school. I've been dating Mitch for a long time and it would probably be good for me to be "normal" and date guys my own age. I don't know why I'm so confused. I wish I had a crystal ball to tell me what the right decision is. Why can't life be just a little bit easier?

**12/2/90**

I can't wait to leave home to go to college. Mom has been bugging me lately. I can't even really put my finger on what it is. I just feel like I want to get out of here. I'm tired of having curfews and rules. In 6 months I'm going to be living completely on my own, it's ridiculous to have to be treated like a child now. But "as long as I'm living under their roof". . . this sucks!

## 12/30/90

Xmas was good. I got a lot of stuff for college. It's making me excited to go. Gregg asked me to go shopping with him on Xmas eve to buy presents. I was so excited that he asked for my help. I think we are getting closer and I love it. Gregg dressed up as Santa on Xmas eve (I dressed as an elf). It was my brother's idea, he went out and bought the costumes and everything. I don't know what's gotten into him. It's like he's so much more appreciative of our family since he's been away.

Jill and I are sort of slipping apart. It's been happening for a while and I think I just didn't want to deal with it. But I think she is doing drugs. I don't want that as a part of my life. I've tried to talk to her about it and help her, but she just lies to me. I just can't be around her right now when I'm still trying to deal with my own shit. I've got to surround myself with healthy people, not ones that are doing such destructive behavior. But I feel so bad like I'm abandoning her. She stayed with me while I was throwing up (and even joined in with me sometimes). Am I being a bad friend by not sticking with her? I don't know.

Kyla and I are becoming a lot closer. She is healthy. She doesn't do drugs or starve herself or anything. I think it is good for me to be around her and she has been a really supportive friend too. I'm so lucky to have her, it makes getting through things a little easier.

# LINDA'S DIARY

*January 18, 1990*

I am just realizing how valuable these diaries can be as Tara and I were talking last night and tonight about her hospitalization. Anyhow things are generally better . . . 2 wks ago (approx.) she cut her wrists with glass from Mitch's picture. Since then Lou and I stopped working nights after 6:00 (except when he's away and going out to dinner on Wed. nights—agreed upon before Christmas—but Lou and I did not follow through with). Tara has been better since she went to the school counselor (Dr. Lopus) with me and changed classes and expectations. Tonight she baked a B'Day cake for Mitch and found he left Oakland without telling her. She was even not terrible with that, until Justine (from hospital) called—brought back lots of feelings and memories.

*April 22, 1990*

Tara went to Palm Springs for the day yesterday—got back at 1:00 (curfew). She and the others were so afraid of being late (road work was being done on freeways) that she ran so hard, tripped on a sprinkler and fell on the driveway. She said she had a really good time—looking for boys etc.

Louie and I stayed in Santa Maria Fri. night—a Xerox dinner so we took our time coming home as Tara was gone anyhow.

She's doing quite well (I think) with her life etc. Mitch was over

Fri. night for dinner, but I guess they are still officially broken up. He graduates from college next month.

Gregg went to Hawaii for Spring Break. Got back last Wed.

Earth Day today.

### June 29, 1990

Louie left for San Diego for a vacation . . . a few days to see Gregg. I can't sleep. We had a little tiff last night so I slept fitfully and I don't like it when he leaves, especially on the motorcycle.

Tara continues to struggle with Mitch and her friends but overall seems to be doing much better—more expressive and certainly more willing to confront her father. But I always did see her as the only one who could confront him and get away with it.

I'm just getting over something . . . had CAT scan, blood tests, etc. for the dizziness that came on strong over 5 wks. ago and hope I don't get again!!

### Sunday, July 8, 1990

Tara will be on TV in an hour—we're getting ready to tape that.

[Author's Note: Tara was on a local news show appearing with her therapist to speak about eating disorders. She had just turned 17 years old.]

She went to a Richard Marks and Wilson Phillips concert last night with Mitch (for her birthday). He took her to dinner on her birthday as well . . .

Gregg bought a new pickup truck a couple weeks ago.

Tara is banging on the wall—gotta go.

*August 28, 1990*

Gregg is 21 years old today! Wow! I thought last night about when labor pains started and the rest of the night and day. He is a man.

Tara had about 10-12 ASG [Associated Student Government] members over last night. They were practicing a song from Grease for freshman orientation on Thurs. The music was loud, they were all so cute and very much teenagers—so wonderful to see and hear! If she could have seen herself as she is now 8 months ago!

*August 29, 1990*

"Summer Nights" from Grease played for 25th time tonight—still cute—all the kids are still practicing.

Gregg called tonight. I didn't talk to him on his b'day—I understood and remember my 21st as if it were . . . well not too long ago. He's excited about going to Rio for Winter Break—is confused about life, his future, school, etc.

*September 29, 1990*

Tara is angry and doing her adolescent thing—she wants to drop Spanish 4 (having a hard time) and I want to talk with her counselor first to see if this is the best option as she is preparing for college entrance applications.

I realized that she's never been grounded (except for being sent to her room as a child)—she came close this week with Louie—just because of her snotty behavior. She was a joy to raise until this last year. I guess we're getting what we should have gotten all along. I'm almost counting the day until she leaves (I'm sure she is too). I think the reason this is—sometimes—is to protect us from the pain we went through when Gregg left—she's unconsciously taking care of us and herself from that pain. I'll still miss her, of course—but not as much—kids are sure smart.

### October 14, 1990

Betty [a close family friend] came over for dinner last night and Tara and Mitch stopped by to see her . . . They looked really cute together even if it's still hard to see Tara with someone.

Louie got a car phone and is so pleased with it. I don't think he expected to have so much fun with it. He called Gregg yesterday while we were driving around town—Gregg sounded jazzed at Louie's getting it. I miss Gregg—we'll be seeing him next weekend in Las Vegas. I wish he could come home though.

### Sunday Morning, December 1, 1990

Tara had a rough few days this week. For apparently no reason she became moody, depressed, angry . . . this happened after her Wednesday therapy. Louie was out of town—coincidentally. It seems like this happens whenever he is out of town. She told me, among other things, that she's been angry for a long time because I'm a therapist with her and not Mom—I said I think that is me and she is pissed because of who I am.

I've come to terms, pretty much, with many of my faults. I don't like them, but after so many years of trying to change yourself and hating yourself for who you are, you sometimes come to terms and stop fighting inside yourself. For the most part I am at peace inside and that surprises me. I certainly didn't think I'd ever feel this way. There was so much self-hatred for so long. I do hate some of the things I do, or don't do, but that feels different.

I worry about Tara sometimes, I wonder if she will be able to overcome these feelings she has—I'm sorry she didn't get from me what she needed. But I also know that I gave her everything I could.


*December 26, 1990*

My mom and Aunt Lois just left to go home. Louie went to work.

What a lovely Christmas!

Gregg has been here for 6 days. He and Tara totally surprised us on Christmas Eve by dressing up as Santa and elf to hand out the presents. They were so thoughtful and sweet—I went to bed that evening and cried tears of joy. I felt so completely overwhelmed. To see the two of them shopping together, playing together as adults warms my heart beyond words. They participated in singing

Christmas carols in our traditional Christmas Eve ride to look at lights—no complaining or fighting—it was the greatest gift they could give me. Louie was patient and acted polite too—no incidences of anger outbursts. It felt like everyone tried to give me the perfect Christmas and they did. They have all finally stopped complaining about my little traditions (like toasting at the table) and instead of fighting me about them, they have all given in and adopted them and even have gone a step further into creativity (like dressing in a Santa suit!).

## TARA'S DIARY

### 2/1/91

Kyla decided she is going to stay at home and go to Moorpark College. I'm kinda jealous, I think I'd rather stay here too sometimes. But everyone says if you have the grades to get into a good 4 year school you have to go. So I wouldn't dare stay here, and I don't want to keep living with mom and dad. But I don't want to leave Mitch. There is no way our relationship is going to survive. And I don't want to lose him.

### 3/22/91

I hate Mitch, I hate my mom. I hate everyone!!! Mitch and I had another fight. He treats me like crap. I should just leave him. My mom tried to talk to me about it tonight. But I don't need her trying to be interested in my life on her time. She is never there for me any other time, so I'm not gonna give her the time of day when she is ready. I am not one of her clients—she can't schedule time to deal with me.

## 4/21/91

The trip up north was a disaster. Mom and I fought all weekend. I just can't stand the pressure she is putting on me. She loved UC Santa Cruz, couldn't stop talking about how she would have loved to have gone to a school like this.

I hated SF—I'm so confused. I don't know what to do. I will feel like a loser if I go to Moorpark College, but I don't feel ready to leave home. And yet it's like my parents are pushing me out of the house.

## 4/23/91

I think I've decided to go to Cal State Long Beach. I have no idea why. Mom and I had a terrible trip up north to visit colleges. We fought the entire time. On the ride home I just wanted to jump out of the car. And I think mom wanted to strangle me, she was so mad at me. I don't know why I was such a bitch. I'm just so sick of hearing her talk about how great UC Santa Cruz would be. I don't fit in there. If I go there I'll come back with arm pit hair down to the floor. The girls there are totally granola. And it's too far away.

Dad really wants me to go to SFSU, but just cuz he likes the city and wants an excuse to visit. I had actually decided to go there until I went to visit it. It's a total city. It's gross and scary. The school is ugly, there are bums everywhere—no thanks. Gregg wanted me to go to SDSU and follow in his footsteps, but everyone knows that's just a party school and I want to take college more seriously. Besides I need my own school, my own identity. I wish everyone would just shut up. And I guess now they have to.

**4/28/91**

Prom was last night. It was good except Kyla and I are in a fight and it hurt me so much to see her there with Rob and for us not to be talking. It seemed like such a big event that we should be experiencing together. Mitch and I only stayed through dinner then we left to go to the hotel. It was actually pretty boring and uneventful. I thought prom was supposed to be a big deal. Whatever.

## LINDA'S DIARY

*January 23, 1991*

Just a note on one obnoxious teenager whom I'm counting (at times) the days 'til she leaves home. "Don't lecture me, Mother. . . . You don't trust me. . . . I'm eighteen and can do what I want . . ." (she's 17½) .

She is so moody, grouchy, bitchy lately—demanding too. "I don't like you and Dad, so there."

I know in my head she needs to do this, but it is not pleasant. The last months before "freedom" are closing in and she's spreading her wings (knocking her parents in the face in the process). Of course I don't think she's really doing anything awful—drinking a little, skipping some classes, and ???

*January 29, 1991*

Tara has been a shit lately (still)—my head says this is a good sign, my body wants to kill her. She is making us out to be terrible people—easier for her to leave home.

Louie is angry with me and vice versa.

Tara bought "Brides" magazine this week and has been "planning" her wedding. Are we going to pay for this before college? Instead of college? Who knows?

*March 22, 1991*

10:30 PM—Tara just came home in tears (again). "Why would I want to talk to YOU!" was her response to me.

Louie is at school—got a speeding ticket last night and is really stressed out with all he's trying to do.

[Author's Note: Louie started graduate school at Pepperdine University in 1990. He continued in his job during the day and worked toward his advanced degree on a part-time basis. He graduated in 1992 with a Masters in Business Administration.]

We're going skiing in Mammoth Monday—have had lots of glorious rain (and snow). The mountains across from our house are breathtakingly beautiful with tons of snow.

*April 16, 1991*

Tara and I are going to UC Santa Cruz and SF State this weekend to check out campuses. She picks up her $295 prom dress tomorrow + $50 shoes.

We are poor (a joke) for now—after paying taxes and my business is down this year—the whole country is slow.

## Sunday April 21, 1991

Tara has been crying (again)—is lying outside by the pool on the cement—won't talk to us, of course. Problems between her and Mitch, I guess (what else). This almost feels unbearable for Louie and me at times—to watch her suffer so and be so helpless (and a part of the problem too).

She and I came back from San Francisco a day early—she got moody and scared in SF. I had it with giving, giving, giving . . . (money, effort, etc.), so we packed up and left town. She didn't talk to me for 3 hours—fell asleep. Finally, as I was prepared for her to not go to college, or anything, she woke up and we started to talk— it helped. When we got home Lou went out for some food with us, and we talked some more. She is scared about changes, scared to leave home, scared to stay—doesn't want to go to the Jr. College, but doesn't want to go away either. She is so confused and I don't know what to do to help her—probably nothing (staying out of it— which is difficult to do).

She told me she tried to kill herself in 5th grade by stabbing herself with a fork. She said she told me before but I don't remember (I should remember something like that). Louie told her last night (teasing) he hoped he could live long enough to see her suffer through having a teenage daughter.

Prom is next weekend—will she go?

*April 22, 1991*

Tara came home last night from being gone all day—announced now she wants to think about going to Long Beach State or San Diego.

I'm angry—Louie is too. I feel used and abused. This is normal I know—I want to tell her all her options, except Jr. College, are withdrawn—she's not ready to go away. I don't want to be paying for her to stay in a dorm when she'll really be with Mitch. All our fears have come true. Things may have to come to a head. This could get more awful before it gets better.

She got A's and 1 B on her report card and I don't feel like recognizing it. (She gets out of school at 1:30 and her last class is typing.)

*April 23, 1991*

Of course things are difficult—when was the last time I wrote in here daily? We talked to Tara last night—she ended up in tears. Lou and I both talked beforehand about not dumping on her—she probably still feels like we did. She doesn't seem to see or own any of her own behavior and how this affects others. I didn't get up yesterday or today to fix her breakfast (maybe childish). Perhaps if she sees me as an asshole it will be easier to leave—that's not the reason—I figure she's been too well cared for and I'm tired of doing and not getting any appreciation. I don't think she eats the breakfasts I fix a lot of the time—never says thank you and she leaves the dishes for me to clean.

I've been tearful in the past 2 days—part anger, mostly hurt. I know it will be hard to let her go (Oh boy tears!)—so it's easier to get angry. I so very few times have felt angry with Tara it seems strange. My body feels a dull ache that I can't seem to rid—it's been hard for me to concentrate at work—I'm just going through the motions. I talked with Silvia yesterday at lunch. It helped to release some of my frustrations. Pam hasn't been home to call. This weekend (prom) I expect will not be ideal. Louie will be gone on the cruise anyway—but Tara is under so much stress (self-inflicted) it will be a miracle if it gets pulled off.

[Author's Note: Louie and I were scheduled to host a Xerox group on a three-day cruise. Tara's prom was the same weekend. I stayed home to be with her while he did his work/fun duty on the cruise.]

### Friday, April 26, 1991

Tara is staying overnight at Rachel's b'day party and going to Conejo Valley Days tonight. Louie is on a cruise ship to Catalina and Ensenada (sp?). I'm home alone! Tara is supposed to go to prom tomorrow. I say supposed, because she was crying last night—Louie was worried about her when I got home from work. Before I went to bed I got up to check on her (she went to bed—crouched in a fetal position on top of her bed—refused to talk to Louie or me).

She wasn't in bed. I looked for her and couldn't find her. I told Louie just as I was going outside in my robe—found her in Mitch's car—Louie was getting his pants on to come looking for her. Our stomachs have been in knots for at least a week. Louie told me "keep an eye on her this weekend"—which of course I can't because she won't even be home. I'm sure he is afraid she could again get suicidal—he didn't say though. She doesn't talk to us anymore (in some ways that is a good sign—but just doesn't feel good).

Well—we'll see what tomorrow brings.

*April 27, 1991*

Prom! She made it! I was surprised when this morning Tara actually seemed to want me around. We went to get flowers (they were wilted and we had to have them changed). Her nails were done yesterday and beautiful. Her hair took 2 hours. Tara came home and complained that it wasn't right (just insecure). We took lots of pictures, she talked to Louie, who called from the ship, then talked to G'ma Rio. Mitch came over—his vest was too big and I ended up sewing it at the last minute. More pictures and then she left—I cried (surprise?). I then talked to Pam [my best friend] for an hour on the phone.

## LOOKING BACK

## TARA

Throughout my senior year, I battled with attaining the separation I needed from my parents that would enable me to go off to college. On the one hand, I was developing a more mature, healthy relationship with my parents, and I wanted to stick around to cultivate it. And on the other hand, the rebellious teenager in me was done following their rules and ready to explore life on my own terms.

I felt like a failure for being scared to leave home. I denied it at the time, but looking back, I now recognize that I was probably not emotionally prepared to live at the university dorm. I still had not received all the nurturing I needed to get before feeling comfortable enough to spread my wings (in fact, I'm still not sure I've received it all). I felt like a baby bird being pushed out of the nest, and I resented my parents for not wanting to keep me at home. Even though it seems unreasonable to me now, at the time I once again felt rejected and abandoned.

At least it seemed like my recovery was progressing. I was able to stop purging in January 1990. After that, I occasionally still restricted, which I believed I could rationalize as not being hungry. I knew that restricting was not a healthy way to deal with my depression, but I also knew that it was different from the addictive nature of purging.

In July 1990, my therapist was being interviewed on a local Santa Barbara talk show. She invited me to come along with her and share my eating disorder struggles and recovery. I felt honored that she considered me well enough to give advice to anyone else. I happily went along to the taping. Mom seemed so proud to see me on television, which I didn't understand considering the subject matter I was discussing.

Even though I was doing better, I was angry that there wasn't any literature on the market for teens, written by teens, on the struggles I faced. So I began writing a "book" on my experiences and healing process. This project augmented my journal writing activities and served the same purpose of providing me with a forum to express my thoughts and feelings. This partial book stayed buried in my computer, until I unearthed it years later and transformed aspects of it into what you're reading today.

## LINDA

During this time period, I vacillated between feeling elated with my daughter's personal growth and feeling terror that she may not survive this struggle. I didn't know how to set the right limits for her. I hated her angry attacks at me, but at the same time I knew they were a sign of her growth.

Conflict was never anything I felt comfortable with, so I would do almost anything to avoid it. I now believe it is not possible for me to confront deep interpersonal issues without some conflict. I have come to respect, even relish, conflict and its role in my family's growth. Avoiding conflict only made things worse for our family. Finding healthy ways to face it continues to be an ongoing struggle for us.

## CHAPTER 8, MAY–JULY 1991
## A MOMENT OF CLARITY—AND GRADUATION
*"If I want to lead a happy life, then I'm the one who has to make that happen."*

As I prepared for graduation, I gained more and more confidence. I continued to experience bouts of depression, but I also continued to go to my therapy sessions to deal with them. We spent a good amount of time preparing me for college and the new environment I was about to face. Since I had never done well with change, my psychologist was aptly aware of the struggles going away to school could create. As the summer came to an end, we were developing some closure, agreeing to end therapy when I left for college.

The summer before college I continued to work at the local pool, lifeguarding and teaching swimming. Mitch found a job near my parents' home. We spent a lot of time together, dreading the day our long-distance relationship would commence.

My mom and I continued to struggle over fairly typical teenage issues. I wanted more freedom and responsibility; she wanted to maintain her role as my mother. Yet she also seemed eager to have me out of the house. It seemed like she and Dad had all these big plans and were just waiting for the day I left.

## TARA'S DIARY

### 5/17/91

I had the weirdest experience today. I was watching Oprah after school just like I normally do. But today there was this woman on the show who had a really big effect on me. She was an expert on relationships and she was on the show to help families that were having problems. And of course she was smart and helpful and pretty. But it was her sense of self that got to me. She seemed so confident and well-spoken and comfortable with herself. I was sitting there watching her in awe. I want to be like her. I want that calm sense of who I am.

I'm starting to realize that nobody can save me. If I want to lead a happy life, then I'm the one who has to make that happen. I don't know why this is such a new concept for me. It's like I've been playing the victim, wanting everyone to feel sorry for me. And I think I've been waiting for someone to "save" me. I wanted someone to convince me that I was good enough to be in this world, that I was valuable to society. But nobody can make me believe that if I'm not open to believing it myself.

I'm not going to tell anyone about this little epiphany (is that the right word?). It sounds so dopey that I got this new outlook on life from an Oprah show. I'm such a loser! I go through a year and a half of therapy and it takes a TV show to open my eyes to the possibility of my future. I just hope they stay open long enough for me to at least finish college.

### 5/24/91

I've been doing pretty good lately. I've held on to the strength I got from Oprah last week (which really surprises me). I feel energized today. I feel like at least I have a focus of where I'm going.

This last year I feel like I've been roaming around in the fog, stumbling my way through my junior year. I've felt half dead, even these last few months of therapy when I'm supposed to be getting better. Most of the time I just feel exhausted. I feel mentally drained and physically depleted. And I've been struggling to figure out what I'm working towards. I've been so afraid that being cured equals being fat. But I think now I might have a model of what healthiness looks like. I want to be that strong, smart, secure woman.

I want my dad to be proud of me. He always talks about how well I would do in the business world. He says I'd be great at sales and that I have better communication skills than 90 percent of the people he deals with everyday. It's actually pretty neat that he is so encouraging. Especially considering I've been an unmotivated walking zombie the last 2 years. But today I think I'm believing that maybe he is right. Maybe I can make it through college and do well in the business world. When I was little, I used to believe I could be anything I wanted to be. The sky was the limit. I don't know what happened to me. I think junior high was the beginning of the end. It's like I left 5th grade as a happy healthy child and by the time I left 8th grade I hated myself, my family and pretty much the world in general. My self-esteem just got demolished in 6th and 7th grade. Growing up sucks!

The family situation is doing pretty good. We are keeping to our Monday night dinners. I dread them all week, but when I'm there I actually enjoy myself (most of the time). And usually afterwards I feel like a huge weight has been lifted off my shoulders. It's really weird. Even when I don't think I have anything to discuss with them. We just sit down and start talking and all these things come up. I don't know where they come from, but obviously it must be good that I'm talking about them because I feel better afterward. I'm sure my parents hate the Monday dinners. Last Monday was so uncomfortable at first. Dad was angry about work (as usual) and Mom looked like she wanted to be a million other places than at Oak Tree West. But by the end of the night everyone seemed relaxed and more at ease.

Things with Mitch are going pretty good. Although I still doubt the way he feels about me. I'm so confused. Sometimes it seems like he really does love me, but then he goes and does something like forget to call me or break a date to "hang out with the guys" and I just hate him for it. It's like it just destroys me whenever that happens. It sends me into a huge depression. Why do I get so affected by him? Why can't I just live my life and not be so dependent on him for my happiness? I hate it. I feel like every day I'm just waiting for the next bomb to drop—the bomb that sends me into a 2-day depressive trance. And I have to still fight the urge to throw up after he breaks my heart for the 50th time. At least when I had throwing up I had a place to release all my pain. The throwing up took that pain away and made me focus on something else. Now I'm just left with the pain and no way to deal with it.

I get more depressed now than I ever did when I was throwing up. I still sometimes struggle to understand why it was so bad. I know it was unhealthy (physically), but maybe I was better off emotionally. I don't know, regardless I'm not going to go back to that. For no other reason than I know how hard it is to stop. I can't go through the stopping again, it was way too hard. I'll become a drug addict, alcoholic, sexaholic, anything else before I'll go back to an eating disorder. I worked too hard to get rid of that disease.

## 6/17/91—Graduation Day!

I'm graduating high school today . . . yeah!!! I'm really excited. I just feel this intense energy. And I think my parents have a cool present for me. They've been real sneaky around here lately.

I've been so pissed off cuz I have spent the last like 9 months researching cars, insurance—doing all the responsible things to make sure I was making a good decision. I decided I wanted a used RX7—it is just perfect for me, it fits my personality. I asked my dad to just help me out a little bit with it, I was still going to pay for most of it. And he considered it for a while and then one day he just said stop looking for cars it isn't going to happen. Seeing how they have been acting I have a suspicion he might have gotten me a car—I'm sure it won't be my beautiful red RX7, but I know it is a nice present—an amazing present whatever it is. I will be grateful—I just really wanted my car.

Oh well, gotta go get ready. I got a pretty new black dress and cute heels so I better go put them on.

## 6/18/91

Oh my god. I can't believe what my dad did for me yesterday. I love him so much right now. After the graduation ceremony mom and dad came and hugged and kissed me. Then dad gave me a piece of paper with a riddle on it. It was the beginning of a scavenger hunt that would end up taking me all over town searching for clues. After hours *of hunting for my graduation present, the last note, which I picked up from the local In and Out Burger, said:*

The hunt is finally done
I hope you've had some fun
We're proud of you on this fine day
And so your gift is in the driveway
Remember the car you wanted?
Well forget what I said
I bet I know what you're now thinking . . .
Gee I hope it's RED!

*Now of course I was thrilled to see my new RX7 sitting in the driveway with a big red bow on it. But what really means a lot to me is all the effort my parents put into creating this surprise for me. Now I know why people say actions speak louder than words. This totally showed how proud of me they were and how much they love and care about me and my feelings. Are they trying to make it hard for me to leave them to go away to college???*

## LINDA'S DIARY

*Thursday, May 2, 1991*

Almost a world record that Tara has been in a "good mood" from Sat.—until today—she's pouty, won't speak to us, etc. now. We got home from work and she was typing her book on the computer—usually a sign she's depressed or ? (I don't know she doesn't say anymore). She said last night I nag and I have been nasty—probably a little true—in response to her abuse to me the week prior. I can never tell her to clean or do household work without her getting angry—but she's always been that way.

I leave for Oakland tomorrow—CAMFT [California Association of Marriage and Family Therapists] conference.

### May 11, 1991

Saturday morning. We had a Xerox party last night—chili cookoff. I didn't feel good about the house, food—just not enough time, money, effort for things to be the best that I like. I wonder sometimes just where the money does go. My car is old, Lou's is 5 yrs. old, our yard is a mess, the house needs painting, the drapes need to go, the furniture (much of it) is old/handed down. Oh I'm just complaining.

### Sunday, May 12, 1991

Mother's Day—a lovely, relaxing day. Louie took me for a motorcycle ride to Malibu. I lay in the sun while Louie studied. Tara fixed dinner and Mitch was here too. Gregg called again just as we finished dinner.

### June 2, 1991

We got Tara's graduation present over a week ago and I've spent so much time fantasizing about it. I'm driving myself crazy. I've gotten the money's worth just with imagining her face—or what I hope will be her face—some worries about if it's right. I know it is not perfect—but the best we can do. I'd take it in a heartbeat if she

doesn't want it. She and Mitch are still having problems—
ever-present age differences.


*June 19, 1991*
Last Day
*for Tara*
*My little girl will leave me today.*
*The memory will remain*
*as I too left long ago*
*it is for all much joy, part pain.*
*As she ventures forth in cap and gown*
*she has become a woman unto her own*
*not a child, not a baby.*
*Oh, my how she has grown.*
*Just as the butterfly only stays for awhile*
*to complement the flower, to sun its wings*
*to gather strength for a journey*
*to see such wonderful things!*
*The butterfly returns from time to time*
*to share its adventures, to ponder the flower.*
*Then it must travel again to spread beauty,*
*and wonder, in delicate power.*
*She left me.*
*As she must*
*sustain the cycle, continue the plan.*
*To herself, to god, to the world we all entrust.*
*HAPPY GRADUATION TARA*

_July 1, 1991_

Tara's 18th B'day—bittersweet for me—just one of many celebrations/excitements in the last few weeks. We went to Charlie Brown's for dinner, took Mitch. Tara ordered lobster. It was quite a celebration. Graduation went as well as I had fantasized, which is quite well. She and Mitch of course are again talking of breaking up.

## LOOKING BACK

### TARA

As silly as it sounds, the realization I experienced while watching the _Oprah_ show was a pivotal moment in my recovery process. It was like a light bulb went on in my brain. I suddenly had a vision of what I wanted my future to look like and the newfound resilience to get there. I think timing was everything. I was at a point in my healing where I was moving away from the hopeless role of a victim and looking for the next step in recovery. I was searching for an image of what healthy looked like. And that day I believed I found it.

I continued to feel trepidation about starting college and just wanted to get there and find out what it was all about. I felt confident that my eating disorder was long behind me, but I worried about being exposed to the issue at my dorm. I knew I would be faced with girls who were actively engaging in unhealthy eating habits, and I wasn't sure how I was going to deal with that.

### LINDA

Tara and I spent much of this time tensely counting down the days until her departure from home. By the time summer rolled around,

I could hardly wait for her to leave for college. It became a joke that when she wanted to talk to me, she would "summon" me by banging on the wall between our bedrooms—so typically adolescent, but I finally got used to that. Our weekly dinner outings became our family therapy and probably saved all of us.

Louie and I had talked a little over the years about what life would be like with the kids gone. After the last 2 years with Tara, I think I was just tired. I really hoped that putting a little space between us would help ease all our tensions and give her some room to grow up. I knew that once she left home, our lives would change. I didn't spend much time planning wonderful adventures for Louie and myself, however. I knew I would grieve. In spite of how she viewed me, a lot of my self-image was involved in being a mother. I wasn't quite sure how to see myself any differently. I needed to let go before I could see something beyond.

## CHAPTER 9, AUGUST 1991–JULY 1992
## FRESHMAN YEAR OF COLLEGE

*"I was so sick of them when I was living with them, and all it's taken is a week for me to want to be right back in that house."*

In the fall of 1991, I finally left home for college. The process of selecting a college had been horrible. I felt like everybody was telling me what to do and what not to do, from parents to teachers to friends. Everybody wanted something different for me.

My mother wanted me to go to University of California, Santa Cruz. She loved the area, the style of the buildings, and the prestige of a UC school. Dad wanted me to go to San Francisco State University. He enjoyed the city and wanted an excuse to visit it more often. My brother wanted me to follow in his footsteps to San Diego State University. While I was accepted to all of these schools, I chose Long Beach State. Why? Because that was the one school nobody wanted me to go to. Of course, in the end, I hated Long Beach and dropped out after my sophomore year.

Instead of the animal house–type of atmosphere I expected, my first months of college were lonely and scary. I hated my roommate and therefore never wanted to be in my room. I spent hours wandering around the massive campus watching the energetic coeds socialize, all the while feeling empty and longing for home.

I went home every weekend and dreaded Sunday nights when I would have to return to school. Mitch continued to build his career during the week and spent the weekends playing house with me. The time apart made us appreciate each other more. I think he was certain I would find a new boyfriend in college, but I had completely closed myself off from the dating world. I constantly longed for the comfort of home. I now realize that I was not ready to go away to school. But I did not want to shatter my parents' dreams for me.

Looking back, I wish I had attended San Diego State and had the opportunity to bond with Gregg. I could have learned a lot from him. Beyond academics, I needed to discover how to have fun and appreciate life. I believe my brother could have been instrumental in helping me do this, if I had only given him the chance.

## TARA'S DIARY

### 8/15/91

*I have been so bad about writing this summer. I guess I don't really want to write as much when things are going okay. I have been lifeguarding and teaching at Agoura High School. All the people I work with are already in college so they've been telling me stories and giving me advice all summer. I think I'm going to rush. I don't see myself as a sorority girl, but everyone keeps saying that it's hard to make friends in big schools and there are a lot of benefits to joining— like parties, support, etc.*

*I'm nervous about moving out. I don't want to leave Mitch, but maybe it's best for us right now since we don't know what we're doing.*

I'm sure once I'm away at school we will break up. There is no way we can keep a long distance relationship. We can barely handle an in-town one.

I've identified "fat days." There are certain days that I just wake up and look in the mirror and just see fat. Or I'll be walking in the mall and pass a mirror or store window and want to almost die—I look so huge. My therapist seems to think that my body is not really changing that fast from day to day (she has a point there) and that what is actually happening is I'm feeling crappy about something—maybe I did bad on a test or somebody said something that hurt my feelings or something and I translate that hurt into fat. It sounds a little crazy but I think she might be right. I'm going to try to start paying attention more to what's going on inside me on the fat days to see if I can identify what she is talking about . . . we'll see.

### 8/18/91

I've pretty much packed up my stuff. Part of me is so excited. Mom got me the bedspread I wanted and the towels I wanted and they got me a word processor so I can do my schoolwork on it and keep up my journaling. I like having all this new stuff. I feel like I'm starting over somewhere. I'm going to a place where nobody knows me. Nobody knows that I had an eating disorder, nobody knows how fucked up I used to be (maybe still am). But then I'm also scared to death. How am I going to be able to be apart from Mitch? I'm gonna miss my mom too. I get this lump in my throat every time I think about saying good-bye to her. I hate good-byes. I feel sick to my stomach talking about this—I'm gonna go.

**9/5/91**

I can't believe I made it here. I'm sitting here alone in my dorm room. It's so weird. It's like a whole different world here. I feel somehow free yet also very scared. I'm all by myself here. There is nobody to run to when things get tough. I have to just depend on myself. And I don't have faith that I will be able to handle this.

My parents dropped me off last weekend. It was strange saying goodbye to them. I knew it was going to be difficult, but I felt so ready. Yet when it came time I couldn't help but get tearful. It was so uncomfortable. Mom and dad were standing around, not really wanting to leave, but knowing they couldn't and shouldn't stay. And as soon as I saw mom's eyes fill with tears it sparked the same wetness in my eyes. I wrote them a letter about 2 weeks ago. I knew I wasn't going to be able to say the things that I wanted to say to them. I didn't want a huge emotional experience, but I wanted them to know how much I love them and appreciate their support. I miss them a lot. I was so sick of them when I was living with them, and all it's taken is a week for me to want to be right back in that house. There is just too much quiet time here. I don't want to be alone with my thoughts. My thoughts are bad, they are not healthy. I'm used to keeping busy so I don't have to deal with myself. But it's really different here. Everybody is going through this deep introspection. Part of me is excited by this self-discovery environment, but I can't deal with the silence.

I'm so scared about everything here. There are so many people—so many different people. I keep having nightmares that I can't find my classrooms and I'm late for all my classes. I don't know why, I spent my first 3 days here walking around the campus making maps of where my classes are. I feel like an ass pulling out my map in the middle of campus, but I feel like even more of an ass when I walk into the lecture hall late to find 300 faces glaring at me (not to mention 1 pissed off professor).

**9/29/91**

I haven't made a lot of friends yet. I absolutely loathe my roommate. She is a freak. I thought I had problems, man this girl is whacked. So if she is in the room then I try to leave and go be anywhere but here.

I'm starting to meet some of my suitemates but I can't picture ever being close friends with them. We're all so different. And there is already one girl who I guarantee is anorexic or bulimic or both. She is obsessed with the way she looks and constantly talks about how fat she is and how she never eats. I can't be around people like that. It's not healthy for me. Just my luck I have to live with her.

**10/14/91**

The sorority thing is going pretty well. At first it was really weird, all the dumb crap we have to do. Handshakes, songs, rituals . . . not really my thing. But I'm starting to become closer with some of the other pledges and it really helps. At least I belong to something in this sea of unknown faces.

[Author's Note: I joined Delta Gamma sorority during my first weeks at college.]

I have to fight the urge to go home every weekend. As it is I'm going like every other now. I know I won't make as many friends if I'm never around. But it's hard. I need to connect with my old life a lot. I miss Mitch. Long distance relationships suck!

**11/18/91**

I got into a fight with Julie today. I don't know what the hell happened to me. We were in Kristen's room and just sitting around chatting with all the mates. And she started in on how fat she was here and there. And it is so obvious she is just fishing for everyone to say, "No Julie you aren't fat at all, you are the skinniest one here."

I just started yelling at her to shut up and stop talking about the way her body looks—that there were more important things in life and we were all sick of hearing it from her. She was so pissed. She started yelling back at me like who the hell did I think I was and she didn't talk about it all the time . . . blah blah.

I was sort of out of control, but I was sure all the other girls would back me up. We have all talked behind her back about how sick of her we are. But none of them said a goddamn word. I feel so betrayed by them. I feel so alone right now. Conflict makes me so uncomfortable. I feel like I want to throw up. And I feel like a huge fat pig today. I ate so much at the caf. And the only food they have there is fattening stuff. No wonder freshman girls get dorm butts. How could we not with the food we are forced to eat. It's a conspiracy. Kristen told me that the caf workers spray this oily fat stuff on the lettuce—so even the healthy food isn't really healthy.

I want to go home. I hate it here. Now I don't even want to go out of my room cuz I don't want to see anyone. And this stupid word processor is a piece of shit compared to the computer at home. I've

*already lost 2 papers I was working on since I've been here. Okay 1
was my fault I got up to answer the phone and tripped over the cord—
which of course came out of the wall and shut the frickin thing down.*

**12/23/91**

*I'm home for Xmas break and back on my nice computer. Oh how
I've missed this thing. It's good to be home. I don't want to go back.
But I have to because I have this teacher's assistant job so I can't stay
here for the whole month. I'm so bummed out. I feel like I belong here. I
want to drop out of school, just so I can come back up here, but there
are no colleges around here. My parents would never let me.*

## LINDA'S DIARY

### August 3, 1991

Well, this really sucks so far! Louie left this morning. Tara is
camping and Gregg left for a concert. Sometimes being alone is OK.
Not today. I know part of this feeling is the premonition of a month
from now when both kids are gone. I have to get a hobby.

### August 7, 1991

Last night a seemingly insignificant (to the outside observer)
event happened that felt monumental to me in my relationship with
Tara. She called, asked me if she could spend the night with Mitch
tomorrow after the Chicago concert. I said I didn't feel comfortable,
but I needed to think about it—she said she knew I'd not feel good
about it. I decided to let her.

When she came home she sat on my bed. I told her my decision (that it logically made sense, even if my "motherliness" said no). She looked at me and said she had already decided not to argue with me and accept what I said. It was a moment, brief, where it felt like we came together not as mother and daughter, but as adults. I didn't have to treat her like a child and she didn't have to resist back against her mother.

Maturity, for both of us.

I think only a mom would understand. Maybe there is light at the end of the tunnel.

*Wednesday, August 21, 1991*

Tara leaves for Rush Week today—will be gone until Monday. I have been PMS for days and on the verge of tears too (which isn't a normal part of my PMS). I thought I'd feel less bad (proper English?) than I do—that because of all the struggles with Tara that I'd breeze thru this period of letting go. Ha, ha. I now know that after having Gregg here all summer I'm going to miss him too as much as if he'd never left (almost) and yet, I will be glad to get control back of the house. That part I am looking forward to.

*Monday, August 30, 1991*

Gregg is gone—back to San Diego—left early this morning. I've been busy cleaning his room, bathroom and trying to keep myself busy. I cried a little—not as much as if I'd been awake when he left.

I think that was by unconscious design on his part—also, his behaving like a shit for just the last 2 days—makes it easier for all of us to part.

Tara comes back from rush tonight—we saw her yesterday when we (yes) rode down there to take her a dress to wear for her last night.

I rather hoped I could avoid all this midlife/empty nest crisis crap, but I should know myself better. I'm much too sentimental/emotional (even though I'm getting more and more feedback that others don't know this).

I've already been feeling sorry for myself, envious of my daughter (she's got her whole life ahead of her and gets to do what I never could, etc.), my life is over (really dramatic). What do I have to look forward to now—my 1 major job in life is done— what could possibly take the place of raising children? On and on and on.

One part of me knows and understands what all of that is about—it's change, it's going into another phase of life, it's me holding onto the past, it's melodramatic, it's PMS, it's facing a life I do not know/have never known (without kids) . . . it's scary, sad, new. The other part just feels hurt, lonely, left out, old (getting older by the minisecond and that's all to look forward to).

When I get really dramatic I picture Louie and me retiring to our rocking chairs now to sit and wait for the children to come home for a visit, etc. How depressing! The fact is, more than for Louie, this is a transition that I have to go through, all the intellectualizing in the world can't stop. . . . I never have done easy transitions, why should this be any different? I guess I should expect that dying will be quite an ordeal too, not a quick, simple passing. Oh, so much to look forward to.

There are some positive thoughts too. I truly am looking forward to having the house to ourselves, privacy, a sense of freedom . . . and less housecleaning.

*September 2, 1991*

We took Tara to school yesterday at about this time. The tears kept coming in uncontrollable waves, one minute I'd be fine, the next minute an emotional mess. I did try my hardest not to let Tara see—until the end when she gave me her card. By the time we drove out of Long Beach I was fine—the dorms, the kids all looked better than I'd anticipated. I got wrapped up in wishing I was the one going away to school.

I asked Louie to take me to Westwood after. I needed not to go home right away.

*Tuesday, September 3, 1991*

I still feel awful. It is a physical feeling. Yesterday was terrible. Louie and I just wandered around the house—neither of us wanted, or could, talk about it. I think he was mad at me for not instantly being happy—I don't know. The reality of the year ahead has hit—

Lou in school and overworked, the kids gone, no $. One day at a time. It is still better than most people have it right now. I am thankful that I have the chance to feel the pain, the pain of parting—many have never known the joy necessary before the pain.

The house is clean (except for dog hair) at last. I spent yesterday cleaning Tara's room, bathroom and doing my billing for work.

Gregg called yesterday—got Tara's phone #—that was nice— made me cry a little to talk to him. I wanted to hear from Tara, but knew I had to let her call—she needs to go through her own process of letting go. The only 2 phone calls we got all day we both ran for—in hopes it would be her. Today is her 1st day of college classes—we'll probably talk to her tonight.

### Wednesday, September 4, 1991

It was a little better yesterday—until Louie said to me, "So, how does it feel not to be a mother anymore?"—the first real tears of Tues.

Tara called—doesn't get along with her roommate.

Work is my salvation right now, but I need more—time will heal. I know that.

### Friday, September 6, 1991

I'm not crying anymore—just feel bad (incredibly) at unpredictable times that come up unexpectedly in a wave. I can feel it in my chest. I sit in Tara's room sometimes, just sit there—not Gregg's because it doesn't look, feel, like Gregg after redecorating and having it as a guest room for several years.

I have been exercising more than usual—good to deal with the feelings with a positive result. I'd like to go out and spend money I don't have—buy stuff to try to heal the pain.

*Monday, September 9, 1991*

Louie had expectations, hopes, that I'd suddenly turn into a free spirit, instead I'm still the same negative, dull person I've always been. Lately, my writing in here is vaguely reminiscent of my diaries from my teens and twenties. Oh dear, how depressing.

Well, Tara has been gone 1 week. She called last night and said she was "a little down."

*Wednesday, September 11, 1991*

Yesterday, I went an entire day without that feeling, the empty, heavy feeling in my chest. I go into Tara's room every once in a while and just sit. There are no more tears. These stopped after the first day or so. The house stays clean, there isn't much to do. I'm still trying to find the thing to occupy my time. One complicating factor is that I'm broke. So far I don't think I'll make enough to pay my expenses this month—oh, it's only the 11th—there is hope.

*Monday, September 16, 1991*

Tara called yesterday. She's "down"—broke up again with

Mitch. She's sick with a cold again and homesick. Friday Louie had lunch with her and she was doing good.

I called my mother last night. She broke her leg last week and never thought to call me, her daughter. Such a close family. I told Louie I feared I would behave similarly with our kids, not because I want to, but because of what has been modeled to me.

*Friday, September 20, 1991*

Tara came home last night! Not for good (I hope)—she's out with Mitch now. Louie is in San Francisco. The dogs went crazy greeting her and she loved it. We had lots to talk about—well, she did at least. It was wonderful to touch her again and see her smiling face (oh I'm tearful again).

*Friday, October 4, 1991*

See, I really am feeling better—a couple weeks since writing. That's always a good sign. I just read a note Tara left on my bed thanking me for making her pregnant nun costume for tonight's "Good, Bad and the Ugly" costume party at school. If it is one thing both my kids have learned very well, it is how to give appreciation (I just hope they don't feel pressured into it—bad guilt—but comes freely from the heart)—anyway I got a tear in my eye. She seems to be happy at school, especially with the sorority— that all warms my heart so.

Louie is tired, physically, mentally drained, and gone and

busy a lot. I hope he makes it and it's worth it. I do care about him so.

## December 26, 1991

Another Christmas. This one was like no other, less tradition, less magic, a grown-up Christmas. Both Gregg and Tara were bored to death and both had "loves" they wanted to be with. Tara waited all day for Mitch to call to say he was coming home (from his parents' house) and Gregg pined all day for Jackie. These are transition years. I was feeling sentimental, but when it came time for Gregg to leave early (Christmas night to go see Jackie, without enjoying my pie), and Tara to spend the night with Mitch, I was fine. I was OK. I guess I realize they didn't need to be here, that it won't be like it was, and that's OK. They are going to leave and have their lives. Maybe they will occasionally come back, maybe not. Either way, I have got to let them go.

Next year, if it's just the 4 (3) of us, I've made a resolve to not cook and have a repeat of this year. Remember this. We can't eat all the food, Louie and I are getting fat, and I wasted food and that's a crime.

## January 9, 1992

On our anniversary this year: argument and it looked like we would spend the whole day not talking, but we pulled it off. It ended up OK—maybe we have gotten more mature.

# TARA'S DIARY

### 2/2/92

*[Author's Note: The following is original poetry I wrote for my mom's forty-second birthday.]*

**For My Mother**

February 2, 1992

by Tara M. Rio

I left her this year, as I must, sustain the cycle; continue the plan.

I left her as my daughter will leave me years from now.

Concentrating so hard on letting go, I've forgotten the reasons

why it hurts so much to leave.

The latter years of home life full of distance.

Love present yet hidden by the pain and confusion of adolescence.

Our deepest connection made through the bunny stories.

Metaphorical bedtime stories that taught me some of my most

important lessons in life, and helped me get through my toughest times.

Those stories told out of love, each filled with the

intelligence, imagination and warmth of a woman who described

herself as cold.

But now I must leave and break the bond of intense love and hate. She

left me once, a long time ago.

Have I ever forgiven her for wanting to be more than my mother?

Will my daughter ever forgive me for following my dreams?

The pain I felt the day she left me is the pain she now feels

every time school calls me back.

As I move into adulthood our relationship evolves into a mature

friendship.

And the pain I felt from that first working day is now surpassed
by the loneliness and desire for a mother's nurturing love.
Yet only now that I begin to see her as a person and not just
my mother does the pain seem to fade.
Soon I will have a daughter and one day I will leave her as
every mother must.
Then I will find out which pain is worse . . .
leaving my mother
or
leaving my daughter.


## 4/16/92

Haven't had time to write in months. Finals are coming up and I am
so stressed out. This year has been tough. That 8:00 Marine Biology
class is kickin' my ass. I just can't drag myself there that early.

There is no way I'm going to get all A's. I might even get a C. I'm so
stupid. I just don't get science stuff—it's like a block in my brain. Why
is it so hard for me? I'm not used to struggling with schoolwork and it's
making me nuts. My comm. classes on the other hand are pretty much
a piece of cake. It just seems to click with me. My roommates get so
irritated with me cuz I hardly ever study and always get A's on tests
and they study for hours and end up with B's and C's. But if I can do so
well in some classes, why can't I do as well in the others? Maybe I'm
just lazy and don't want to take the time to put in the effort. Like my
dad always used to say I do a half ass job with things that don't
interest me. Whatever!

**6/2/92**

I'm so glad to be back home for the summer. I have missed Mitch so much. It's weird being back here in my house. My room is starting to kinda not feel like my room anymore—it's kinda sad. Dad says I have to knock from now on when I come home at night. What the hell is that about—knock to come into my own house. Dad said he and mom might decide to have sex on the dining room table and don't want to be interrupted. Grooooosssss! They are so weird. But they are being pretty good about curfew and stuff. Basically I don't have one. They said I've been living alone for the last year and doing fine and I'm an adult and can make my own decisions. It's weird, but I'm usually home before my old curfew anyway. I just like knowing that I can stay out as late as I want. It shows that they trust and respect me.

**7/16/92**

I'm trying to figure out where I'm gonna live next year. I thought I was going to live in the DG house, but it looks like it's gonna be all full. Which is okay cuz it's in a bad area of town. I think Mary, Erica, Tricia and I are going to try to find an apartment together. It should be fun. I like Mary and Erica a lot. I don't know Tricia that well, but I'm sure we'll all get along fine. I'll have to make some trips down to LB to look for places the next couple of weeks. Part of me really doesn't want to go back. It's been so nice seeing Mitch every day—or almost every day—actually pretty much when he has time for me.

## LOOKING BACK

### TARA

My transition to college was lonely and difficult. However, with each month, I gained the confidence and security to forge on. I guess this is a lot of what college is all about—learning how to survive on your own.

During my college years, I began to interact with my parents on a more adult level. I experienced a lot less anger and our interactions became respectful once again. I appreciated the freedom and responsibility they were giving me.

I could see a sense of relief in their eyes when I would visit home on weekends. I had survived high school and appeared successful in college. Their dreams for my future seemed to once again resurface after being tucked away during my illness. I wanted to be happy, if nothing else just so I could continue to please them. But I was still quite confused. I wanted to want to be away at school having fun and learning new things, but I just didn't.

I had come to a crossroads in my relationship with Mitch. After almost 4 years of dating, neither of us was satisfied with a long-distance relationship anymore. There was a deep sense of tension in the air. It felt like we couldn't continue on the path we were on. We both knew we had to choose a direction to proceed in. We needed to decide whether to finally break up and move on from each other or fully commit to our relationship.

### LINDA

The transition into Tara's college years was slow the first few months. I grieved. I didn't know what to do with myself. But I also liked having a clean house to come home to at the end of the day, and I started to enjoy my house and garden more.

Of course, I worried about Tara's eating disorder and depressive obsessions. I tried very hard to let be what had to be, let her have her own life. She was emotionally very up and down. I never knew what to expect from her phone calls from college or during her occasional trips home. I reveled in seeing her involved in sorority life. When she was "up" and "on," she was a delight. But the "down" and "ugly" side of her was there, too.

She would sometimes tell me about the other girls in the sorority and express her concerns for the eating disorder behavior she saw there. I worried about a relapse with her being in that kind of environment. But she and I talked about that, and I had to believe her when she told me that she'd let me know if she was in trouble.

It was easier to allow Mitch into the family once Tara graduated high school. The age difference between them really bothered me initially when they started dating. He was fully an adult and she was just 15 then. Once she was 18, however, it just felt better to let her decide for herself. I never had anything against him anyway, except for his age. I grew to love him, especially as the years went on.

## CHAPTER 10, AUGUST 1992–MAY 1993
## THE COURAGE TO GO ON
*"Something really bad happened to me, but it didn't kill me. And I learned a lot from it."*

In the fall of 1992, I returned to Long Beach State for my sophomore year of college. During that school year, an event took place that would become a turning point for me.

On February 12, 1993, my diary tells about one of the worst events in my life. Eight weeks earlier, I had been sexually assaulted. Immediately following the incident I was unable to write about it. Somehow seeing it on paper would have made it real, and I was still trying to pretend that it didn't happen. It took all the courage I had to write about that night. But as I look back, I think that my ability to survive that ordeal—and write about it—was an important element in my recovery from the eating disorder. Despite the trauma, I survived. I knew for sure that nothing, not even this attack, could cause me to relapse.

## TARA'S DIARY

### 8/6/92

*I'm anxious about going back to school. I've been depressed all week. I just don't feel like I really belong there sometimes. Thank god* for the sorority—at least it gives me some sort of network to belong to.

I've been having a fat week! But I think it is because I'm feeling down about leaving again and stuff. I hate change—it is so hard for me. I don't know why I have such a hard time with it, but I really do. It throws me for a major loop. How am I going to survive this long-distance relationship? I don't want to do this for another 3 years.

**9/3/92**

I'm rooming with 3 other DGs this year. I don't really like our apartment. It wasn't my first choice, but we were running out of time. It's not in the greatest area of town, but it's nice inside. I'm sharing a room with Tricia—we'll see how that goes, she's already buggin' me. I think I'm gonna like my classes this semester. I'm taking interpersonal communication—my professor is so amazing. The class is in a huge lecture hall, so it's really not very interpersonal, but I think it's going to be sooo interesting. I'm starting to get into my major classes now, which are so much more interesting.

**9/22/92**

I was elected Foundation chair for the sorority. It's pretty cool. I will be handling all the philanthropic work—which can be boring but at least it's something meaningful. I'm kinda proud to be heading up the 1 area that's not all about parties and superficial crap. Nobody else really wanted this position, but I'm going to really try to do a good job with it and get people inspired to help again.

**10/15/92**

Erica, Mary and I are becoming really close. Tricia is bugging all 3 of us and I wish I was rooming with them instead. She comes home from the gym dripping with sweat and lies down on my bed and talks on the phone for an hour. Get your own damn bed all sweaty and gross. She thinks I am such a bitch for asking her to lay on her own bed. Whatever!!

**10/26/92**

I organized a clothing drive—to give to the Long Beach Homeless Shelter. It's not our main charity, but I thought what do we have that we can give to the community—well god knows these girls have clothes— they throw out clothes that are just a few weeks old. So I thought instead of having them all go to waste we should bring them to the shelter. It was a huge success. I had so many bags of clothes I couldn't fit them all into my car. The girls got so excited about it. I got such good feedback on the event—it makes me feel really good.

**11/14/92**

I think Kyla is going to come visit me. It will be nice to have a piece of home down here. We don't talk as much now that we're both in college—kinda leading separate lives. It will be nice to spend some time with her again—sort of like high school again. I don't know what the heck we are going to do though. Neither one of us has fake IDs and there's nothing to do in this town without an ID.

I've been having a lot of fat days lately. I don't know why. I know I'm supposed to look inside myself to figure out what's really bothering me, but I just can't seem to see it lately. There is nothing obvious going on, but still I just feel yucky.

[Author's Note: On December 12, 1992, I was sexually assaulted during a weekend trip to Tijuana, Mexico. The next few entries reflect my state of mind as I tried to tell the people around me—and my diary—what had happened.]

## 12/20/92

I don't think I'm gonna make it. After everything I've been through and I'm still going to end up killing myself anyway. What a waste of time and money. But I just can't get through this. I'm trying but it's not looking good. I'm not sure I can write about this yet. It's just too difficult.

## 1/5/93

Well I'm still alive . . . at least that's what they tell me. I don't feel alive. I feel completely dead inside. I have gotten so bad that I actually went to see the counselor at school. It was so embarrassing walking into the student center to go see her. But I really like her a lot. She is very nice and compassionate and I think she may help me get through this. She has encouraged me to keep writing; she says it will help me process what happened to me. I'm going to try, but I can't yet.

## 1/16/93

I told mom about what happened to me. She is such a bitch. I don't even think she believed me. She had absolutely no compassion at all. Like I caused this to happen. If I was one of her fucking clients she would never treat me this way. I made her promise not to tell dad. I don't know why I even try to talk to her, I never get what I need from her.

She's just not the warm comforting person I'm looking for. Why, why isn't she what I want—she is a mother—mothers are supposed to be nice and caring and want to take away all your pain. I will never act like her when I'm a mom. I'm going to tell my kids I love them every day and make sure they know that I will always love them no matter what they do or say. I will give them lots of hugs and always listen to their problems and try to help them get through tough times. If I ever have children that is. I will probably never get the chance, especially now. Now I'm just ruined.

**2/12/93**

Okay, I'm ready to talk about this. God if anyone ever reads this I will die. Kyla came down to visit me here at school a few weeks ago. We were sitting around my apartment just so bored. It's not fair all of our friends are either 21 or have fake IDs. They can all go out to bars and have fun and we have to sit at home like little kids.

We thought it would be fun to go down to Tijuana since you only have to be 18 to drink there. I was kinda scared about going just the 2 of us, so I called Mitch and asked him to go with us. He said he didn't want to—didn't feel like driving yadda yadda. So Kyla and I went alone.

It was so fun at first we walked into this bar and everybody's heads turned (I don't think they get too many blondes in Mexico). Anyway from just about the minute we sat down men started sending drinks over to our table. We thought we were in heaven we didn't have to pay for anything. We were so stupid we just started throwin' those drinks back.

A group of marines came over to our table and sat down. I don't remember things really well, all I know is that as the night moved on this one marine started holding my hand then putting his arms around me. I have to admit I liked him at first. I even gave him my address cuz he said he really wanted a pen pal—he was so lonely sometimes, etc. I got pretty out of control, I was dancing up on the bar—having a great time and this guy started getting really possessive of me—grabbing me away from other guys when they wanted to dance with me or talk to me.

All of the sudden I felt like I was going to throw up. The room was spinning—I was really messed up. I told him I needed to rest somewhere or I was going to be sick. He said oh I'll take care of you come with me. Kyla saw me leave—she was talking with his friend the whole night. I didn't even have the sense to make sure we stayed together or anything.

Anyway this guy took me to a motel near the bar and paid the front desk (I think he even took money out of my wallet to pay for it). He walked me up the stairs (because I could barely walk at this point) and he opened the door. We walked into the room and as soon as I heard the door shut behind us he threw me down on the bed and started pulling at my clothes. I was in such shock at first I don't even think I moved. Then once I realized what was happening I tried to push him off of me.

He got my tank top over my head and threw it across the room. He quickly unbuttoned my jeans shorts and started pulling them down. At the same time I was trying to keep them up. He pulled my hands off my shorts and pulled them down, panties and all. He threw apart my legs so hard and then he lay on top of me and tried to kiss me. I kept turning my head from side to side so I wouldn't have his lips on mine. I was so terrified I just kept thinking oh my god he is going to rape me I can't believe it I thought we were friends, I trusted him.

He started unbuttoning his jeans and he pulled "it" out. It was already totally hard and that's when I began to really panic. He tried to stick it inside me and all I kept thinking was don't let it get inside . . . don't let it get inside. I didn't want to get a disease or get pregnant and of course he didn't put a condom on. I cupped my hand and held it over myself down there. He kept thrusting into my hand and yelling at me to move it. It was almost like a sick game. He was trying to hold one of my arms up over my head while trying to guide his thing with his other hand, but he would have to use that hand to pull my hand away and when he did he'd put his hand back on his thing to guide it in and by the time he did I'd have my hand back in place to cover it. He finally gave up after I don't know what seemed like a half hour but I'm sure was really only a few minutes or even seconds.

Then he dropped to his knees and pushed my legs apart and started kissing me down there. I kept trying to throw his head away from me, but he'd come right back. I couldn't squeeze my legs together hard enough. He was so strong. I would try to get up and move, but just one of his arms down on my chest kept me in place. I felt like I was in one of those dreams I sometimes have where I'm trying to run away but it's like it's in slow motion and I'm not going anywhere. No matter what I do or how hard I try to run I just don't move. That is how this felt. No matter how hard I pushed his arm up he didn't budge. No matter how hard I tried to push my legs together they wouldn't go. I felt so helpless. He was a marine for gods sake I don't know why I thought I could have any effect on him. He was trained to assault people. I didn't know what the hell I was doing.

Thank god Kyla and another marine started banging on the door and yelling for him to open up. He stopped and I grabbed my clothes and threw them on. As soon as the door opened I ran out into the streets. I foolishly thought I would be safer on the streets of Mexico.

Kyla and I finally made it out of that god awful city that I will never return to. But I don't think I got out unscathed. I have been an absolute fucking mess. I'm scared to leave my apartment. I sit in here and run around checking the locks on the doors and windows. All I do is go to class and that's it. I don't even know how to explain my emotions. I'm only actually being able to talk about this because of the therapy sessions I've had. The first week after I came home I tried to forget it happened. I tried to tell myself that I imagined it even though I knew I hadn't. Then I went to the mailbox after class and saw a plain white envelope with unfamiliar handwriting. My heart fell into my stomach. I felt like throwing up (how appropriate) right there on the sidewalk. I slowly walked into my apartment debating on what to do with the envelope. I decided I had to open it. I don't know what I thought I was going to see—some sort of apology is I think what I was hoping for. Instead he wrote me like nothing ever happened. Told me how nice it was to meet me and how he had a great time and hoped we could continue to keep in contact. He ended the letter by saying "P.S. you were the best midnight snack I've ever had." I had such a sudden rush *of anger. I took the letter into the kitchen and lit it on fire. I just sat there watching it burn in my sink, hoping the smoke detector wouldn't start sounding. And then I sat on my counter and cried and cried.*

*I started looking around at the knives in the kitchen and imagining how each one would feel on my wrists. Which one would do the job the best. Which would be fastest, hurt the least. Should I blow out the pilot light on the stove? No I don't really know how and I don't want to blow up the entire building, what if other people got hurt. I felt like I had to talk to someone about it but I didn't know who. I remembered hearing about some rape crisis hotline, but of course I couldn't remember the number. I hunted around for the phone book and found a number. I was shaking as I was dialing the phone. A woman answered the phone and I almost hung up except she had a hint of compassion in the way she greeted me. I told her that something happened to me, but that I hadn't been raped and I probably didn't qualify to use this number. She asked me to tell her what happened and I did. Not in great detail, but the basics. She said that I had been sexually abused and I had every right to call this number anytime I needed to. I guess that's all I needed to hear, that there was someone out there that I could reach out to if I absolutely had to. I hung up shortly after and the call was short, but it gave me the strength to not try to kill myself. Although every day since then I've been struggling to find a reason to stay alive. I feel like damaged goods. I feel like it is my fault. I know it's my fault. I voluntarily kissed him. I talked to him all night long. I danced with him. I was in a foreign country drunk. Of course this was going to happen to me. Why was I so stupid? And how could one night destroy me like this. Why can't I just forget about it?*

### 3/11/93

I miss Mitch. I go home every weekend and I just want to be there with him, where I'm protected and taken care of. I hate it down here. I hear gun shots outside my window and there are bums everywhere. I don't know why I didn't notice it as much last year. But I'm still alive. Physically at least.

I've just tried to focus on going about my normal life. Routines help me get through. I desperately look forward to my counseling sessions, it's the only peace I get. I desperately need to process all this crap. I'm still so embarrassed and ashamed, I'm so glad I have my counselor to talk to. She says what happened to me is very common, especially among college girls. She said date rape—which I guess is what kinda happened to me—happens to many girls. This somehow makes me feel better, which is terrible really. It's not that I want a lot of girls to go through this, but it's nice to know that I'm not alone. She is giving me hope that maybe I can live through this. Which is funny cuz my first reaction was just instantly "I have to die, I'll never make it through this." I didn't think I was strong enough (and I'm still not sure) but if I've made it this far I think I have a shot. The worst has to be over, right?

### 3/28/93

I signed up for self-defense classes. I just decided I couldn't spend the rest of my life afraid of my shadow. I hate it. I never used to be like that and I don't want to be. I won't let that asshole ruin me. I know no matter what they teach me I won't be able to fight off a 6-foot marine, I'm just hoping for a little more confidence when I walk through a parking lot. I'm really doing this more for the emotional reasons than anything else. School's going better. I got A's and 1 B last semester and I think I might get all A's this one.

**4/2/93**

I love my self-defense classes. The instructor is just amazing. He used to train with Charles Bronson or something. Anyway I really feel comfortable with him—he is the first man (besides Mitch) that I have felt that way with since "the incident."

Sorority stuff is going well, although I'm probably not participating as much as I should. I don't go to any of the parties. The last thing I want to do is hang around a bunch of drunk frat boys—that is just an "incident" waiting to happen.

Sometimes I don't know what I'm doing here. I want to go home, I want to be with Mitch. I went to the beach to study yesterday and all I could do was watch these cute young moms playing on the sand with their kids. I want that to be me. I feel like I'm ready to start my life. Mitch keeps talking about how we should just get married, and I'm starting to think he's right. It's been almost 4 years now, we know we want to be with each other. But my parents will kill me if I drop out of school to get married. My mom will kill me. Because I'll be making the exact same mistake she did. What she doesn't realize is I wouldn't view my children as a mistake—I want kids right now. I wouldn't resent them for taking away my youth.

**4/13/93**

I'm so excited my self-defense instructor asked me to join the kickboxing class. He said I have some really good skills and if I want to take it a step further I should continue to work on it. So now I go even more and I'm learning so many cool things—karate and boxing—all stuff that makes me feel stronger and more secure. Pretty soon he's going to let us start sparring. I can't wait.

### 4/20/93

I got a black eye. I thought I was so cool in the ring boxing. And I was doing pretty good for a while, especially seeing how I was fighting a 6 foot 200 lb man. Then wham I got a right hook to the face . . . didn't see it comin'. How am I going to explain this one? Truthfully I'm pretty proud of it. I got a boxing injury!!!

### 5/2/93

Well school is winding down. Finals are coming up and I'm pretty stressed about them, but I've really enjoyed my classes. I feel good. I can't believe I'm actually saying that, but I think it's true. I thought I was really doing well last year—being in college by myself—doing fairly well. But I can say I'm even better now. Which is amazing because I was a wreck just a few months ago.

I can't believe I actually survived what I went through. Not that it was all that bad or anything, but this is me we're talking about. I don't want to live on a good day. I didn't need any more excuses to hate myself, other people and life in general. But I got through it. I actually handled it pretty much on my own. I reached out for help when I needed it and I accepted it. And I did it all without throwing up once. I didn't become an alcoholic or a drug addict, I just survived. Wow. Maybe it's true what they say about how going through difficult things makes you a stronger person in the end. I would have never believed it when I was deep in it, but I can truly say that going through that terrible experience has made me stronger. Screw him, he actually did me a favor. I was on a slow track to health since the eating thing. And going through that just sped up the process. It was like the last step was finding my inner strength and trusting that I could survive the worst. And I found out (the hard way) that I could go on. Something really bad happened to me, but it didn't kill me. And I learned a lot from it. I learned never to get drunk in Mexico and never to trust a marine—no just kidding. I've learned some valuable lessons about the kind of person I am and the strength of my character. I think I will remember this year and carry its memories with me for the rest of my life.

**5/6/93**

I'm excited to go home. I can't wait to be with Mitch again. I'm sick of it down here. I'll miss the kids I've been teaching, though. They are so great—so loving—all they need is a little attention and to know that someone cares about them and they just flourish—ahh good word. I'm having another fat day, but I think it's because Mitch and I argued on the phone last night. I always feel like crap when we argue.

**5/21/93**

Today was my last day at work.

[Author's Note: I was a teacher's aide at a local elementary school.]

The kids surprised me with a huge banner they made that said "Goodbye Miss Rio, we'll miss you." It made me start to cry.

This one boy Bryan who I have been struggling with all year began to cry and wouldn't go out to recess with the rest of the class. He just _stayed in the classroom hugging me. All year I have felt like I just can't get through to him, but I think maybe I actually did. I always tried to give him a little extra attention cuz it just seemed like he needed it. But I never thought he really noticed, he always tried to act cool around his friends but it looks like deep down inside I may have actually made a difference with him. That makes me feel so good. It's been a long year, but I think I'll remember this day for a long time._

## LOOKING BACK

### TARA

As horrible as the sexual assault was, it served as a self-defining event in my life. Prior to the incident, I didn't believe I was strong enough to handle even the everyday struggles of life. Being pushed to the brink of sanity forced me to fight my way back. It served as a launching pad for a deeper level of healing.

When I called my mom to tell her about the incident, I was hoping for comfort and support. When I didn't receive it, I came to the realization that my mother was not able to give me what I felt I needed, and therefore I would have to give it to myself. This was a revolutionary idea that had escaped me up until that moment. I realized that I could no longer expect other people to fulfill my needs. I had to learn to take responsibility for my own emotions and soothe myself. It was after this that I began to both mentally and physically build myself back up to an even higher level than where I was before the incident.

Even though this event pushed me to rely on myself more, it wasn't until years later that I resolved the unmet needs from my mother. It took the analogy of one therapist to finally break through my unyielding image of what I thought a mother should be. She said to me one night in session, "What you're doing is going shopping at Home Depot to buy milk." My puzzled look prompted her to continue, "Do they sell milk at Home Depot?"

"No," I cautiously responded.

"If you know they don't sell milk there, then why do you continue to go back looking to buy it?"

Once I realized she was not criticizing my shopping habits, I began to understand her point. Over and over again, I went to my mom searching for something she was unable to provide me. I needed to accept the fact that she was physically unable to meet my needs. Instead of continuing to bang my head against the wall, I needed to find other ways to get what I needed. So I began to examine where I did receive the bits of support and comfort I longed for. And I spent time reaching out to my grandmother and girlfriends to fill the void I felt my mom left, as well as learning to console myself in times of need.

I told Mitch that I had been sexually assaulted immediately when I returned home. He was the person I trusted the most. He was also the person I received the most reassurance from. He was angry that it happened and felt guilty for not coming to Mexico with me, as I had asked. But this experience brought us closer together—in part because I now held a deep level of distrust for all other men. I came to believe that Mitch was the only man who would not hurt me. This belief reinforced my conviction that life would be better if Mitch and I were married. It is no coincidence that 6 months later, I was pregnant and we were planning a wedding.

The sexual assault has left an indelible mark on my soul. I continue to hold shame and guilt about my role in it. I haven't totally forgiven myself for allowing it to happen. I still struggle with trusting new men in my life, and I continue to allow fear to keep me hidden away at times. And of all the intimate details I share in this book, this issue was by far the most difficult to release. Allowing it to become public meant I had to finally truly deal with it. I never told my dad about it. I was terrified at the thought of telling him, but I knew he would be more hurt if he had to find out by reading it in this book.

After months of agonizing over how to broach the subject, I finally conjured up the courage to meet with him. Before I was even halfway through my story, he told me that he already knew about it. Apparently, my mom had told him over 10 years ago. However, respecting my need for privacy, he never forced me to discuss it with him. Relieved, I spent the rest of lunch finally sharing my feelings with him. Once again, my dad surprised me by being more sympathetic and supportive than I ever expected he could be, forcing me to learn another valuable lesson about the way I create anxiety over situations that don't truly warrant it.

Looking back, it's strange to read the things I promised to do with my own kids. For the most part, I have fulfilled my vows to tell them that I love them every day and to do my best to make them feel protected and supported. But only time will tell if I've truly succeeded in those goals. There are times when I'm frantically running around the house trying to get things done and my eldest daughter will be trying to share a story with me. Like my mother, I survive life by multitasking. And I catch myself not giving her my full attention. It breaks my heart to think I might be making my daughter feel as unimportant as I did. But sometimes I feel destined to repeat my mom's mistakes.

After my first child was born, I gave up writing in my diary, feeling that there was just too little time in the day. However, after my second daughter was born, I began to keep a journal again. The difference is that now I write entries to my girls. I tell them things they are too young to know right now. And I record funny stories about them that I am afraid I'll forget when they are older.

To this day, my journal acts as a safe haven for my intimate thoughts. I hope one day my daughters will enjoy reading my diary as much as I enjoyed reading my mother's.

## LINDA

These last diary entries of Tara's are some of the most difficult ones for me to read. When Tara told me about the assault, she made it sound like a near miss, not anything as serious as this. She made light of it, and I stupidly didn't probe further to question the exterior she presented. I work with sexually assaulted women every day. I know the devastation this kind of experience brings. I am horrified that I did not go running down to her college, wrap her in my arms, and hold her until she could feel safe. That is what I wish I had done. I could not have healed the wound, but I could have been more of the mother she needed. Another missed opportunity. Thankfully, despite my reaction, she turned it around. She found her own strength, and in the end that is what really matters. I am proud of Tara for getting out of Tijuana alive, but mostly for taking this situation and eventually doing something good with it.

As for the rest of the family, time marched on. Gregg married Jackie, a girl he met while attending San Diego State University. She is a beautiful girl from Rio de Janeiro, Brazil. Gregg started searching for a job after graduating from college. He and Jackie moved in with us for 8 months right after they surprised their families by getting married. That brought a new challenge for all of us—living in close quarters together.

Now that our children were older and we had a bit more free time, Louie and I started riding his Harley and taking fun motorcycle trips. We also started doing more home remodeling projects. It became a passion for me to surround my home life in beauty, serenity, and as much nature as I could.

# EPILOGUE
## LOOKING BACK

## LINDA'S DIARY

*October 26, 2001*

I have to laugh at myself! I haven't changed much at all. Tara has, though, and that pleases me. Something happened today to exemplify just what got us into this mess in the first place. Tara had asked me to set aside time Saturday in order to work on this book idea she has. Since she thinks we can actually write a book together, I am willing to give it a try. She put the kids into the playroom to watch a movie. They were told Mommy and Grandma had a special project we were working on and they should not disturb us. They were not the problem! In my usual distracted way I kept getting up to do laundry, see what the kids needed, talk to Louie, etc. Tara finally looked me directly in the eyes and yelled at me! She said, "I am angry with you. Sit down and listen to me. Mom, this is just what I have been talking about and what the book is about. You never pay attention to just me. I want your attention, now!" She really gave it to me. Good for her. I may not change, but at least she, now, has found her voice.

## LINDA AND TARA

Quite a bit has happened in our family since 1993. There have been weddings, divorces, and babies born, all of which have presented new challenges and enlightened satisfaction. It would be nice to be able to say that we no longer struggle or have arguments, but that would not only be untrue, but also unrealistic. Like any other family, we still have issues to resolve. The difference is, we now have the communication skills and trust in each other to work through those issues.

So what became of us?

About a month after Tara's last diary entry, while cutting the cake for her 19th birthday, she announced to her parents that she was pregnant. With Mitch by her side, the two explained their plans for marriage and family.

After working so hard to mend our mother-daughter relationship, we were once again at odds. Linda's college and career dreams for her daughter had been deflated. And despite her efforts to guard against it, Tara seemed destined to repeat her mother's mistakes and follow in her footsteps.

Much of the progress we had made connecting over the previous few years seemed at risk of coming apart over this. But the difficult times we spent nurturing our relationship saved us. We listened to each other, we took time for each other, and we moved toward accepting each other and our own choices.

Tara dropped out of college after her sophomore year to raise her young family, which was blessed by the addition of Carli 3 years after Ashlee's birth in 1994.

In 1998, Tara picked up her career plans with a new sense of confidence, determination, and success. As her young daughters—and beaming parents—looked on, Tara proudly accepted her diploma in 2000, graduating magna cum laude with a bachelor's degree in communications from California Lutheran University. Tara now enjoys a career as a public relations executive with a Fortune 500 company. She knows she too will make mistakes with her kids, and she hopes that they won't be writing a book about her someday.

While Tara considers herself "cured" and no longer practices disordered eating, she still struggles with body image issues on occasion. When she has a "fat day," she knows she must work through it to find the deeper anxiety or hurt causing it. Even more than 10 years later, she still has to make a conscious effort to not let self-doubt take over her life. But with each passing year, she becomes a little less critical and more accepting of herself. Battling to stop the cycle of self-hate among women in her family, she strives every day to model healthy, self-loving behavior for her daughters to follow. She has publicly shared her experiences with various local commmunities, including eating disorder groups, classes at California Lutheran University, and a conference for therapists. She also assists in the coordination of Eating Disorders Awareness Week activities and communication.

Today, Linda continues her private practice as a marriage and family therapist, supervises therapists in training, writes, and teaches graduate school courses. Maintaining a deep passion for her work, she continues to work long hours—while the family continues to complain about it. She and Lou still struggle with some of the trials of marriage, but they value their unrelenting love and commitment for each other, having recently celebrated their 34th wedding anniversary.

Gregg went on to develop a successful career as well. He and Jackie lived with Linda and Louie for 8 months before Gregg got hired with the company of his choice. They recently celebrated 10 years of marriage and now live nearby with their 6-year-old daughter, Shyann. Despite the intense struggles between Tara and her brother when they were kids, their relationship has evolved into a very close friendship, complete with the bond only siblings share. As children, they competed for the little available attention; they now work together to maintain the kind of close-knit family they both hold dear.

Lou continued his successful business career. He works fewer hours nowadays in a conscious attempt to add balance to his life. He is remorseful about the mistakes he made in earlier years and has learned how to manage his anger in more positive ways. At family dinners together, it is Lou who suggests the dinner topic for the evening. It is he who asks the deep, thought-provoking questions, which sometimes spark heated debates that we've all come to enjoy participating in. As the head of our family, Lou guides us through troubled times and inspires us to live life to the fullest.

Tara and her dad have developed a closeness that they did not imagine possible during her teenage years. To this day, they take time out of their busy schedules to meet after work regularly to re-connect. The father she once knew as angry, stern, and unap-proachable now demonstrates an unrelenting commitment to creating a healthy family. He shares his emotions freely, cries while remembering the pain his family experienced, and lights up as he plays with his grandchildren. Tara always thought of her dad as her hero, and his capacity to accept faults and give all of himself for the sake of his family proves he truly is one.

Tara had always wanted to be "daddy's little girl," but the bond she had always longed for was blocked by her rage and fear. Only after years of working through her anger did she truly begin to feel that she has earned the title that, in reality, she has always held.

After Gregg and Tara moved out of the house, Lou and Linda got the grand idea to take up motorcycle riding. Their lengthy trips on the Harley have added long overdue fun and lightness to their lives. They also enjoy Lou's classic 1947 Plymouth and being grandparents to Ashlee, Shyann, and Carli.

Sometimes there are casualties in the course of recovery, and un-fortunately, Tara's marriage was one of those casualties. Mitch and Tara divorced in 1999. However, they remain very close, contin-uing to talk on a daily basis and sharing custody of their children. They are committed to staying partners when parenting their girls. They have developed a new kind of relationship with the primary goal of raising healthy daughters.

The diary entries included in this book were taken from our family's darkest period. It was extremely difficult to highlight this ominous era, knowing that so much of the happiness and positive aspects of our life would not be represented. But we chose to move forward knowing that our family's triumphs overshadow our dif-ficulties. We would not have been able to share such troubling memories if we weren't secure with the sound relationships we share with each other. Despite, and perhaps because of, the struggles we experienced, we possess an authentic bond that few are lucky enough to experience.

Today, our family is closer than ever. All residing just miles from each other, we work hard at striking a balance between allowing necessary independence and honoring our strong value of family. We all lead busy lives but try, more than in years past, to enjoy life and value fun as much as work. We still meet every Sunday for dinner, which serves as a time when we can catch up, connect with each other, and get grounded before beginning a new week. Through lively, frank, and open dinner conversations, we listen to each other and ensure that we're each heard. Food, which was initially the source of great pain for our family, now serves as a medium for healing.

Our relationship as mother and daughter gets stronger with each passing year. As new generations begin, we share more in common and relate to each other in ways we never could before. Because of our intense struggles during Tara's teen years, we have emerged as stronger individuals and more supportive family members. We may still disagree about our views of reality, but we validate each other's perceptions and respect differing opinions.

We seriously doubted our ability to expose our private thoughts to each other and be so vulnerable during the process of publishing these diaries. Yet, through this pain, we find solace. What once was covered in shame and guilt has been transformed into acceptance, mutual respect, and an even deeper love for one another—proof that sometimes families have to be broken apart to be put back together in a healthier way.

# PART II
## ADVICE AND
## COMMENTARY

Craig Johnson, Ph.D.

# CHAPTER 11

## UNDERSTANDING AND TREATING
## EATING DISORDERS

Helping someone recover from an eating disorder is a humbling experience. As director of the eating disorders program at Laureate Psychiatric Clinic and Hospital in Tulsa, Oklahoma, I can tell you that each patient's case is unique, and effective treatment requires understanding the person's biology, psychology, and family life, as well as the culture he or she lives in. Yet as challenging as treating eating disorders can be for medical professionals, it is even more so for the families of these patients. To family members, the actions of someone with an eating disorder seem mysterious, and the treatment may mean digging up uncomfortable and often embarrassing truths about family life. As you've read in Linda's and Tara's diaries and reflections, the Rio family's experience was painful but ultimately triumphant.

Since Tara first began her destructive eating patterns back in the 1980s, much has been discovered about how eating disorders develop and how they can be treated. Yet many questions still remain. These questions add fear and uncertainty to an experience that is already confusing and frustrating. In the following pages, I'll detail what doctors and researchers have learned about these disorders and offer advice on recognizing and seeking treatment for them in your own family. To help clarify the often complex issues associated with eating disorders, I'll use Tara's experience as an example. Rarely have I seen a case that so clearly illustrates the struggles of a person with an eating disorder and those who love her. (Please note that because the Rios' story revolves around a mother-daughter relationship, I've limited my comments to the female experience of eating disorders and to Tara and Linda's experiences, rather than include how their family crisis affected the male members of the family.)

One of the things that stand out in my mind about Linda and Tara's diary entries was that their experiences were, for the most part, fairly common. Far too many books and TV movies have sensationalized these illnesses, presenting only high-profile or highly dramatic accounts. What makes the Rios' story so extraordinary is that they are an ordinary family in an ordinary situation that any of us could face in our own homes. They react in ways that I see every day in my work.

The other thing that makes their story so noteworthy is that it's being told at all. Family secrets and emotional challenges like the Rios faced and triumphed over are rarely explored with such candor and openness. So, while their story may be ordinary, the courage and compassion that Linda and Tara demonstrate in sharing it are truly extraordinary.

## WHAT ARE EATING DISORDERS?

The two most commonly recognized types of eating disorders are Anorexia Nervosa and Bulimia Nervosa. There's also a third type, called Binge Eating Disorder, though it's not yet recognized as an official disorder. Let's take a closer look at each one.

## ANOREXIA NERVOSA

When people develop Anorexia Nervosa, they become terrified of fat or weight gain. They become obsessed with avoiding fat or losing weight and engage in a variety of compulsive behaviors such as exercising, restricting calories, or purging (either by using laxatives or diuretics or by forcing themselves to vomit).

One of the easiest ways to understand Anorexia Nervosa is to think about it as a phobia. Interestingly, 95 percent of the people who develop phobias have never had a bad experience with the phobic object. Rather, a phobia is an irrational fear of a thing or place. What has usually happened is that the person has experienced an event or a number of critical life changes that he or she found scary or confusing. In reaction, the person becomes overwhelmed by anxiety or depression, which results in them feeling terribly out of control. Because feelings like anxiety and depression are abstract and can be very confusing, the person may find that it's easier to shift their focus to something more concrete, like fat or the size of their waist. Once they shift their focus to this concrete object, the things they need to do to manage their uneasiness become clearer. It also sets the stage for them to be able to use what are called avoidant defenses.

For example, when a teenager experiences a scary life change that she isn't prepared to deal with, she may shift the focus of her anxiety to body fat, believing that if only she were thinner, she would feel better. To feel better, then, she believes that she needs to avoid or reduce fat. To that end, she begins to use behaviors such as dieting, exercising, or purging to avoid and protect herself from the perceived threat, fat. Furthermore, she gains a concrete barometer, or measure, of how she's doing (such as scales, clothing sizes, number of calories consumed, and minutes of exercise). Essentially, she is now using avoidant defenses to try to feel in control. Unfortunately, using avoidant defenses works only temporarily. The person gets brief relief, but then the uneasiness begins to mount again, resulting in the need to intensify the avoidant behaviors. For anorexics, dieting deteriorates into starvation, exercise can become extreme, and purging may begin or intensify.

Tara began her eating disorder with anorexia nervosa. Her descriptions of feeling overwhelmed by nearly every aspect of her life, including the emergence of the disease of depression, is a classic example of what I have just described. In early to mid-adolescence, her life became more complex. As she entered high school, her coursework got harder, her brother left home, and her mother was busy establishing a career. During this time, she felt her parents were less available to help her with the range of new and confusing thoughts and feelings she was experiencing. She felt progressively out of control and reached a point where she felt she was literally "falling apart." In an effort to pull herself together, Tara decided that if she lost weight, she would gain a sense of control over herself. Once she made this shift, fat became the concrete representation of the enemy, and her body became the concrete battlefield where she would fight for control. From that point on, she spent many years trying to find other ways to express herself and feel in control.

## BULIMIA NERVOSA

Patients diagnosed with Bulimia Nervosa have recurrent episodes where they consume large quantities of food in an uncontrollable manner. Following these binges, they then purge, either by forcing themselves to vomit, abusing laxatives, or exercising excessively.

Bulimia is anorexia's sister. The two illnesses are from the same family even though they may look quite different. Furthermore, 50 percent of patients who start with anorexia develop bulimia during the course of their illness. For many bulimics, food actually becomes like an addictive drug that they are compelled to take. While anorexia is similar to a phobia, bulimia is more similar to an addiction.

As with anorexia, bulimia is triggered when a person experiences a frightening or confusing event that leaves them feeling out of control. Like anorexics, bulimics try to restore a sense of control by going on a diet and losing weight. The self-starvation works for a while, but eventually their restraint weakens and they have an episode of overeating. Usually purging behavior such as self-induced vomiting quickly follows the initial episode of binge eating. This "undoing" behavior will actually make the binge eating worse over time, since it gives them license to eat without fear of weight gain, which makes the overeating more and more appealing.

The experience of binge eating seems to be both horrifying and gratifying to bulimics. Like alcoholism, overeating, purging, and excessive exercise can alter a person's neurochemistry and psychology in a way that becomes very addictive. Soon they begin a pattern of secretiveness and dishonesty with their bingeing and purging that alienates them from their loved ones and throws them more fully into their relationship with the illness. They are ashamed and feel terribly out of control, but they are compelled to continue the behavior. Eventually, they are bingeing and purging most of the day. In fact, their world deteriorates to the point where they are bingeing and purging unless there is a compelling reason not to binge and purge.

Tara's descent into bulimia follows this pattern. Initially, she felt some relief through her successful weight loss. Ironically, however, as she became more malnourished, fatigued, and disconnected, her ability to starve herself weakened. Almost instantly after she started purging, her secret began to overtake her life, and she found herself behaving in ways that were unfamiliar and confusing to everyone.

## BINGE EATING DISORDER

Although clinicians have noted binge eating disorder for more than 50 years, it is not yet an official diagnosis, so less research has been done on it. Binge eating disorder is essentially bulimia without the purging behavior. Consequently, this subgroup is usually overweight. Their eating episodes are equally out of control as their bulimic counterparts' are, and they often experience the same level of life impairment from the illness.

There is actually a much larger number of people who are struggling with binge eating disorder compared to anorexia and bulimia. Far more men and older women are affected. My hope is that this will become an official diagnosis in the near future so these individuals can gain access to the care they need.

## WHO IS MOST AT RISK FOR DEVELOPING EATING DISORDERS?

Tara is practically a poster child for the type of person who develops anorexia and bulimia. Ninety percent of the group that develops these illnesses are white females between the ages of 12 and 25. During childhood, most had been "the best little girls in the world." They were bright, successful students and athletes. They were the last kids on the block that you would have thought would fall apart during adolescence or young adulthood. They predominately come from middle to upper middle-class families with caring, well-intentioned parents. Interestingly, less than a third of the girls who develop these illnesses were significantly overweight prior to the illness.

People who are susceptible to eating disorders often fit a specific psychological profile. Certain personality types, as well as predispositions to certain mood disorders such as depression or anxiety, make a person more likely to develop anorexia or bulimia.

## PERSONALITY TYPES

There are two particular types of temperaments that predispose individuals to developing anorexia and bulimia. I affectionately refer to these two different groups as Turtles and Hares. In addition, both Turtles and Hares struggle with what I call "The Toad Within."

*Turtles.* Overall, turtles are temperamentally very anxious and fearful. They are cautious, fearful of taking risks, shy, and very sensitive to rejection. They are often what we call "neophobic"— meaning that they do not like new things. They prefer the familiar. They are very orderly and can be quite persistent and perfectionistic. Finally, they like for things to be more concrete than abstract. They prefer issues to be black and white, rather than vague. People with this temperament are often drawn to anorexia nervosa.

*Hares.* Hares are very different. Overall, they are more impulsive and erratic. They are vulnerable to rapidly changing and highly volatile moods, which can make their lives very chaotic. They are very extroverted and love change. In fact, they can become easily bored if things aren't changing quickly enough. And they can be very oppositional. As you may have suspected, hares are drawn to bulimia.

*The Toad Within.* The Toad Within is low self-esteem. Low self-esteem is the most common personality trait among those with eating disorders. As different as Turtles and Hares might be, this is a shared difficulty. The low self-esteem can range from a moderate feeling that they do not quite measure up to an agonizing feeling that they are worthless and deserve to be punished.

Tara doesn't appear to be an extreme Turtle or Hare. She is fairly extroverted, willing to take reasonable risks overall, and doesn't seem to be overly impulsive or chaotic. She is not an extreme perfectionist or overly fearful of change. She has fairly good balance, so these temperament issues would not be a significant factor for her. Unfortunately, Tara does live with a Toad Within. Despite the fact that she is a very good student, has close friends, and won a spot on the school swimming team, she doesn't think very highly of herself, and her negative self-talk becomes very harsh and punishing. This more punitive form of low self-esteem places her at great risk for an eating disorder and other forms of self-destructive behaviors, such as cutting herself and making poor decisions about boyfriends.

## MOOD DISORDERS

Approximately two-thirds of the patients who develop eating disorders meet the criteria for major depression and anxiety disorders. Half of these individuals had significant episodes of depression and/or anxiety prior to the onset of their eating disorder. In fact, the mood disorder is what provoked the feelings of being out of control in the first place. The dieting, exercise, and purging are then an attempt to fix the feelings of being out of control caused by the mood disorder.

Many of these patients have what we call biogenetically mediated depressive illness. This means that they have inherited the disease of depression or anxiety from a family member, and the disease will begin at a predictable time, the individual will display a predictable set of symptoms, and the illness will follow a predictable course. Persons suffering from depression have little interest in what interested them a month ago. They withdraw from friends and family. They have trouble concentrating and develop sleep difficulties ranging from wanting to sleep all the time to not being able to sleep at all. Their appetite can become chaotic, alternating between having no appetite to being completely preoccupied with food. Psychologically, there is a profound shift in their perspective. The most obvious is an increased negativity. The glass becomes increasingly half empty rather than half full. Everything also becomes a catastrophe. Mundane, everyday events become issues of life and death. They can become suspicious and believe people are out to get them. They can also become very impatient, irritable, and hypercritical of themselves, friends, and family members. Nothing is good enough. Symptoms can come on suddenly, or they can develop over a period of weeks or months.

The disease of depression can be accompanied by deep feelings of anxiety. Anxiety adds a level of agitation to the symptoms described above. It can also be an illness without accompanying depressive symptoms. Many patients with eating disorders struggle with an ongoing feeling that they describe as "wanting to climb out of their skins." It is an extreme form of nervousness that results in them being continuously on edge. Others suffer from panic attacks, which often come out of the blue. They suddenly feel panicky and dizzy, experience a tightness in their chest, and start to hyperventilate. They report feeling like they are "falling apart." It is an extreme feeling of loss of control that provokes an ongoing worry and dread that the symptoms will happen again. The unpredictability of the attacks is often one of the more terrorizing aspects of the illness, particularly if the person affected is a teenager.

As mentioned earlier, there is a very strong genetic component to mood disorders. They run in families, can begin as early as childhood, and can develop without any obvious trigger.

Tara had several family members who had the disease of depression. In fact, one was hospitalized several times throughout her life for treatment of the illness. Further, Linda openly acknowledges episodes of depression in her diary, and there is a good chance that Lou's bouts of impatience, irritability, and criticalness could be understood in this context.

As I read Tara's diary entries, it was obvious to me that she was unknowingly recording her development of biologically mediated depression. The onset and depth of her depression simply could not be explained by events in her life. In fact, moderately stressful, fairly average events, such as her boyfriend not calling on time, became increasingly catastrophic as a result of her worsening depression. One of the tragedies of folks trying to use dieting and weight loss to fix depression is that semistarvation eventually makes the depression and anxiety worse. While psychologically they feel better in the beginning, eventually the calorie deprivation causes a neurochemical interaction that induces more depression and intensifies their negative perceptions.

## OTHER PSYCHIATRIC ILLNESSES

There are other psychiatric illnesses that co-occur with eating disorders. About 40 percent of eating disorder patients will also have Obsessive Compulsive Disorder (OCD). In fact, for a subgroup of these patients, their obsessions and compulsions related to eating are just one symptom of their primary problem with OCD. When we successfully treat their eating disorder symptoms, they substitute another symptom like compulsive hand washing.

Twenty-five percent of eating disorder patients will also have significant drug and alcohol problems. When this is the case, it is usually necessary for the drug and alcohol problems to be treated first before addressing the eating disorder.

Although the prevalence of Attention Deficit and Hyperactivity Disorder (ADHD) among eating disorder patients has not been firmly established, it is clear that a subgroup exists. The use of stimulant medications can be quite helpful to this subgroup. Since the risk of abusing these medications is high with eating disorder patients, it is important that their use be closely monitored.

## GENETICS AND EATING DISORDERS

Recent research indicates that there may be a significant genetic contribution to the development of eating disorders, particularly for anorexia. Studies have shown that relatives of individuals with eating disorders are at substantially greater risk for having eating disorders themselves than relatives of individuals without eating disorders. This is called relative risk. In fact, preliminary studies indicate that the relative risk is 12 for anorexia and 4 for bulimia. This means that if you have a parent or sibling who has had anorexia, you are 12 times more likely than others to develop anorexia. If they had bulimia, you are 4 times more likely than others to develop it. Studies on twins offer further support for the role of genetics as a risk factor. Identical twins (monozygotic) share all of their genes, and fraternal (dizygotic) twins share, on average, half of their genes. If a disorder occurs in both members of identical twins more often than it occurs in both members of fraternal twins, then the disorder can be said to be influenced by genes. Concordance rates (how often each twin has the illness) for identical twins with eating disorders consistently run twice as high as for fraternal twins.

It does appear that there is a subgroup of folks who have a genetically mediated vulnerability to developing the more severe forms of anorexia and bulimia. For these people, rapid or severe weight loss; a diet that deprives them of protein, carbohydrates, or fats; or excessive exercise may trigger a neurochemical response that creates the obsessive and compulsive symptoms of eating disorders. These findings have significant implications for girls who are thinking about going on a diet or beginning a strenuous exercise program. For genetically at-risk girls, these seemingly innocent actions may have disastrous effects.

## WHAT ARE THE MORE COMMON CAUSES OF EATING DISORDERS?

People develop eating disorders for many different reasons. As mentioned earlier, the most common reason is that they are feeling out of control. The dieting, weight loss, and exercise are misguided efforts to restore a sense of control or improve themselves. Virtually every patient I've seen in more than 25 years of practice began the behaviors because they thought it would improve or fix things in their lives. And for many, in the short run, it did make them feel better.

While a single event such as a perceived failure, a depressive episode, rejection by a boyfriend, or sexual or physical assault can cause the onset of an eating disorder, more often it is the result of a combination of things that have accumulated over time. The primary causes include major life transitions, such as entering puberty or going to college, and family problems, such as being unable to connect emotionally with one's father. Let's examine each of these major issues in turn, using Tara and her family as an example.

## MAJOR LIFE TRANSITIONS

Adolescence is a confusing time for even the most well-adjusted teenagers. While they're no longer sheltered as they were when they were children, adolescents haven't yet developed the life skills or experience of adults. Their entire world seems to be in up-heaval—beginning with their bodies and extending to their new-found relationships and responsibilities.

## Entering Puberty

I think that by the time we are old enough to be parents, most of us have forgotten how incredibly confusing and disorienting puberty is, particularly for girls. But as parents, we need to fully respect the magnitude of change that occurs in a relatively short period of time.

The infusion of hormones in early adolescence begins to dramatically affect girls' bodies, thoughts, and feelings. The average American girl is expected to gain 40 pounds in the 4 years between the ages of 11 and 14. Normally, girls will gain about one-third of their adult body weight during these 4 years. In a culture that equates fat with failure, social rejection, and slothfulness, this normal weight gain can be unnerving. Further, the development of sexual characteristics such as breasts and hips introduces a level of complexity, conflict, and danger with both men and women that they have never experienced before.

Perhaps the most confusing and devastating change can be the unconscious withdrawal of fathers and/or brothers in response to a girl's emerging sexuality. Old ways of physically interacting suddenly become awkward and may not be replaced with other, more developmentally appropriate ways of connecting. This is a time when brothers and sometimes fathers can begin to tease girls about their changing bodies. This, of course, is disastrous. Another frightening scenario is that previously safe men in her life, as well as strangers, begin to respond to a girl sexually, either consciously or unconsciously. These new experiences can be profoundly overwhelming, causing a young woman to want to return to a less complicated prepubertal world.

In addition to the outward changes in their bodies, adolescent girls are also experiencing significant internal changes. There will be a dramatic surge in various appetites and feelings. Because pubertal development for girls is dependent upon increasing body fat, hunger is most often the first appetite to ramp up. Most women have to maintain 17 percent body fat to menstruate and 22 percent to be fertile. Essentially, body fat in women is our species' way to control the population. If there is a famine, women's body fat drops and they become infertile. Their fertility will not return until their body fat increases, indicating that the food supply is adequate to support new mouths to feed. So, increasing and protecting body fat is an incredibly high priority for the female body during puberty and beyond. And hunger is the appetite that will be intensified to accomplish this goal. But, once again, this very natural biological drive is at odds with a culture where fat has been vilified. Increased hunger and weight gain can cause teenage girls to feel like they are no longer in control of their own bodies.

Other feelings and appetites that become intensified include sexuality, aggression, and overall mood. Not only do the girls look more sexual, but they feel more sexual as well. Their neurochemistry is pushing them to be interested in men and to attract them sexually. The drive to procreate can be as compelling as hunger. The ebb and flow of hormones during the menstrual cycle also adds mood variability and volatility. Girls who were used to fairly stable moods during childhood find their moods all over the map from day to day and week to week. Girls who were already struggling with mood variability during childhood now feel profoundly out of control.

The most important thing to understand in this discussion is that when girls drop their body fat to less than 17 percent, their hormone levels return to a prepubertal state. They no longer look like an adolescent or have the complex feelings of an adolescent. They are able to return themselves to a childlike state, both physically and emotionally, by reducing their body fat to the point where they stop menstruating. Boys cannot reverse puberty by reducing body fat in the same manner as girls. This is one of the reasons the disease primarily affects girls.

Tara did pretty well with most of the challenges of puberty. She seems to have enjoyed the camaraderie of her girlfriends and the increased attention she was receiving from guys. She didn't seem to be overwhelmed by the intensification of her sexual and aggressive feelings. Her mood, however, appeared to be deeply affected by the biological changes, and, eventually, she developed a diagnosable depressive disorder. In March of 1989, when Tara is 15, she confides to her diary, "I'm so miserable I can't even think straight. I hate everything. I hate my parents. I hate the way I look. I am so fat." As the months pass, her diary chronicles her descent into lethargy and her withdrawal from family and friends. This culminates in her not being able to get out of bed, which is a common end stage of a major depressive episode. Puberty triggered Tara's biogenetic vulnerability to depression, and the depression became one of the major factors contributing to her development of an eating disorder.

### Gaining New Freedoms

Entering high school, learning to drive, and starting to date are major rites of passage in our society. For healthy teens, they signal an exciting time of increased freedom and opportunity. For other teens, however, these experiences can be frightening and overwhelming. To them, they are a symbol of a leap into adulthood—a leap that they feel ill-prepared to make.

When a student enters high school, she is suddenly expected to become much more independent and responsible. The level of protective hovering by teachers and coaches decreases significantly, and the students are expected to "fend for themselves" both academically and socially. Being able to drive also dramatically increases their opportunities to range outside their parents' supervision and engage in activities that their parents might not be able to know about.

For teens who are psychologically robust, this increased freedom is welcomed, and they thrive with the new opportunities. For the psychologically vulnerable, it is a time of new and complex problems. For turtles, the new emphasis on independence can be absolutely terrifying. In fact, anorexia can be a full-throttle retreat from these increased opportunities for separation/differentiation. As mentioned earlier, reducing their weight below their menstrual threshold physiologically reverses puberty, sending them back to childhood, both physically and psychologically. The loss of structure and supervision can be equally devastating to hares. Once they are able to come and go more as they please, they can become very chaotic. The variety of new things they can experience may leave them feeling overstimulated and disorganized. Usually, their eating, sleeping, and studying habits are the first things to suffer. Likewise, girls with low self-esteem are going to be at a high risk for feeling like they can not handle the new challenges and that they are failures.

This is the phase that Tara had the most difficulty with. While she enjoyed being able to be more independent with her girlfriends, her diaries also record her complaints about feeling abandoned. With her brother away at college and her parents distracted by their careers, her family structure began to fragment. She wasn't ready for the level of autonomy that developed, and she became anxious and fearful about the freedom she had. Interestingly, and as often occurs, she filled the gap with a boyfriend. Tara chose an older boyfriend who presumably could protect her from the perils of independent living. He could become a mentor, guide, and coach to help her through the next steps in her life. However, the inequity of their ages and her level of desperateness made her vulnerable to being exploited.

There were several other things that created difficulty for Tara during this phase. Her girlfriends also became distracted by guys, making them less available to Tara for support. Also, when guys enter the equation, a competitive element is often introduced that affects the girls' friendships. Tara also quit swimming during this time. This became a double risk for her eating disorder. She lost the daily structure of the practices, and the additional free time meant additional hours spent alone and feeling lonely. She was also used to being able to eat with some freedom because of the calories she burned while swimming. When she quit swimming, she panicked about weight gain and started purging just weeks later. Once she started purging, she realized that she could eat without fear of weight gain, which then gave her permission to eat more chaotically.

## Moving Out

The next sizable developmental challenge is the transition out of the home, often to college. Concerns regarding college increase dramatically the second semester of the junior year of high school. Taking the ACT/SAT tests concretely drives home the fact that physical and psychological separation is right around the corner. At risk teenagers begin to show signs of difficulty from this point through their freshman year of college. Whatever fears they may have about being able to control themselves outside the structure of their homes can begin to materialize in various forms, including eating disorders.

But why eating disorders? Remember, dieting/weight loss equals control, success, and popularity for girls in our culture. It is one of the ways they can concretely demonstrate to themselves and others that they are in charge of their lives. In fact, the rate of dieting reaches astronomical proportion the summer before the freshman year of college. For some, the dieting takes on a desperate and frantic quality—all under the guise of self-improvement.

This transition also puts substantial stress on existing romantic relationships. For girls who developed overly dependent relationships with boyfriends as a way to become less dependent on their families, the transition to college becomes a double threat. They face losing the support of both their families and their boyfriends.

Tara clearly struggles with this transition. Her choice of a college becomes a complicated and high-stakes battle within the family. The first complication was Linda's over-investment in her daughter's choice of college. After the two take a trip to check out potential colleges, Tara writes, "Mom and I fought all weekend. I just can't stand the pressure she is putting on me. She loved UC Santa Cruz, couldn't stop talking about how she would have loved to have gone to a school like this." Tara feels that her mother is so concerned about her choice of college because she's trying to make up for her own lost opportunities when she became pregnant and dropped out of college. She feels that her mother is trying to fix something within herself through her. This feeling has the effect of throwing her back into a more enmeshed relationship with her mom, at a time when she is trying to more fully differentiate from her. Tara will almost be forced to reject any school that her mother likes in order to hang on to her fragile differentiation.

The second complication is her boyfriend. Unavoidably interlaced in the college decision for Tara is the question of whether her parents will try to manipulate her choice to steer her away from her relationship with Mitch, which her parents have passionately and appropriately discouraged from the beginning. Even if she decides that this isn't their agenda, she faces being away from him if she goes away to school. Since her identity is so enmeshed with Mitch, Tara has legitimate fears about whether she can take care of herself in his absence. The whole business of choosing a school and leaving home becomes an overwhelming mess for her and her parents.

## Going to College

The Rio family's experience of Tara's transition to college was quite normal. Linda and Lou go through that tearful moment when everything is moved in at school and it's time to say goodbye. The symbolic significance of this goodbye is apparent to everyone. It signals a new chapter of development for all. Linda and Lou return home and begin to deal with the fears and fantasies that normally accompany an empty nest. Tara goes through the proverbial realization that her life was pretty "comfy" at home and that she took many of these comforts for granted. She has normal struggles with roommates and her long-distance relationship with her boyfriend.

There were two events that occurred during Tara's college years that deeply affected her development and recovery from her eating disorder. The first was when she successfully organized a clothes drive for charity. This was a step toward letting go of her more narcissistic adolescent values and replacing them with more altruistic ones, and it became a cornerstone for a more positive identity for Tara. The clothes drive was a truly independent expression of her emerging values.

The second event that profoundly affected Tara's healing was the date rape that occurred in Mexico. Unfortunately, this is a particularly common event among young women who develop eating disorders. Approximately two-thirds of young women who receive residential treatment for eating disorders have been physically or sexually abused. Fortunately for Tara, this occurred at a time when she was psychologically "ready enough" to be able to transform the trauma into a growth experience. One of the more important side effects of this event was Tara's reaction to her mother's response to the date rape. Tara feels her mother responds insensitively and ragefully recites, once again, her mother's maternal shortcomings. Then an interesting thing happens. In this moment I believe that Tara unconsciously comes to accept that her mother is not going to be able to protect her and fix all the things that break in her life. Tara uses her rage over her mother's failures to empower herself to find ways to protect herself and fix things on her own. It is a moment of fuller differentiation from her mother. Tara crosses over into the realm of responsibility and accountability for herself. Although trauma is not the preferred path to empowerment, Tara was able to turn this adversity into a growth opportunity.

### The Young Adult Years

Graduating from college is also a high-risk time for many of these young women. This is the time when they are expected to leave the last vestiges of childhood and adolescence behind. They need to become more financially independent, establish careers, and establish or refine long-term romantic relationships in preparation for starting their own families.

Tara was fundamentally in recovery at this point. Although she episodically struggles with minor relapses over the next few years, she was basically ready to take on the challenges of young adulthood. She married Mitch, started her own family, eventually finished school, and established a career. Her marriage ultimately failed, but that is not surprising. Many relationships that develop when an individual is struggling psychologically do not survive recovery. If treatment is effective, people change, and sometimes the changes are not equally comfortable to both parties. Tara and Mitch had the additional burden of being essentially "childhood sweethearts." The failure rate of these marriages is also quite high. To both of their credit, it appears that they shared enough good moments that they are able to continue to partner effectively to parent their children.

## FAMILY PROBLEMS

Parenting children under the best of circumstances is extremely difficult. As a humbled parent of two teenagers, I understand that. So, as we begin to discuss the dynamics within the Rio family, I want to fully acknowledge how much easier it is to calmly analyze a family situation with the hindsight of a number of years than it is to get it right when you are in the middle of the action. I also want to make it clear that most of the parents I've worked with over the years have been concerned, well-intentioned people. They want to be helpful, but they are unsure about what to do if they have psychologically vulnerable kids.

With that caveat in mind, let's examine some of the parent-child and overall family dynamics that can contribute to the development of an eating disorder, using the Rios as an example.

### The Parents' Marriage

It is always important to learn as much as possible about how the family began, because context is important. Lou and Linda's marriage began under difficult circumstances. They became pregnant as teenagers and married probably more out of obligation than a true readiness to enter into a long-term relationship. Throughout their story, you hear many of the common struggles that couples entering marriage in this manner encounter. Concerns about money, although a real concern at one level, are more often a symbolic expression of what they might have been able to accomplish if they had been able to pursue their dreams without the early obligations. Money talk becomes a shorthand communication for the frustration of stunted dreams. Sexual tension is also highly predictable, particularly if premarital pregnancy has happened to "a good Catholic girl," as Linda describes herself. Like money, sex becomes a shorthand communication about how ill-prepared they are as a young couple to navigate the challenges of marriage and parenting.

### The Relationship between Mothers and Daughters

Mothers of girls who have developed eating disorders have gotten a bad rap. They are generally characterized as overprotective and controlling. The truth is that most are trying hard to do the right thing for their daughters. The dilemma is that most girls who develop an eating disorder are having abnormal difficulties navigating the developmental challenges of adolescence and young adulthood. They are overwhelmed by their own development. The daughters' struggles draw attuned mothers into overprotective relationships with them. After all, if your daughter is starving herself to death, it would be neglectful not to become increasingly controlling and intrusive.

Girls who develop anorexia unconsciously accomplish some interesting things with their self-starvation. On the one hand, most anorexics openly acknowledge that taking charge of their food and their bodies is the most independent thing they have ever done. Their "dieting" is an assertive attempt to take charge of their lives. The obvious health hazards of the behaviors will assure, however, that their parents will continue to be very involved, if not overinvolved. The girls essentially "get two birds with one stone": They are able to practice autonomy (controlling their eating and body size) while ensuring that their parents will not get too far away, particularly their mothers.

Linda was 23 when Tara was born. She had a 5-year-old son, the honeymoon was over in her marriage, and she was having increasingly more severe episodes of depression. It was 1974 and feminism was in full swing in California. She had a great deal of permission, and perhaps some peer pressure, to look outside her marriage and family for self-enhancement. Linda's decision to pursue college was a "watershed" event similar to Tara's self-defining event in Mexico. Tara used the date rape to clarify that her mother was not going to be able to protect her and that she needed to take responsibility for her life. Likewise, Linda's decision to pursue college was an acknowledgement within herself that her relationship with Lou was not going to fix some of the self-esteem struggles that had persisted throughout her life. While Linda's decision to go to school was good for her personal development, unfortunately, it also increasingly distracted her from her family.

Linda's emotional distraction is highly characteristic of many of the parents I work with. While these parents genuinely love their kids, they are also distracted by other pressures in their lives. Most of my patients' parents are very successful, which results in them having a great deal of responsibility outside their families, both at work and with other causes. They take these responsibilities very seriously and spend a lot of time worrying about them. Children of parents like these are often getting the emotional "leftovers" at the end of the day. For kids who are not psychologically robust, the distraction progressively deteriorates into a nagging sense of disconnection or emptiness that is hard for the child to describe.

Tara's diary entries are replete with examples of what I have just described. She was finally able to articulate it most clearly while working with her mom on this book. As Linda recalls in her diary, Tara finally proclaimed, "I am angry with you. Sit down and listen to me. . . . You never pay attention to just me. I want your attention, now!"

Tara was emotionally a high-need child. Her moods were intense and significantly affected by her genetic vulnerability to depression and low self-esteem. She was also a "hyper-attuned" child. She was very aware of distraction, conflict, and unhappiness in her parents. Her capabilities, particularly her social skills, were a mixed blessing. These strengths actually allowed her to hide some of the intense feelings that she was struggling with. Yet the more successful she was at hiding her feelings, the more rageful she became that her distracted parents were not able to see how much she was suffering. It would be highly predictable, given this scenario, that Tara would unconsciously become more overtly symptomatic to draw attention to the problems she was masking.

The good news is that Linda was able to overcome her distraction and intervened quickly when Tara's struggles became more obvious. Once this occurred, Linda's attention became riveted on Tara, which at an unconscious level was what Tara was longing for. Then we see the terribly confusing push-pull that develops between Tara and her mom regarding the level of attention Tara wants from her mom. She pulls her in and then ragefully throws her out. In a sense, this is what most adolescents want. They want their parents around so that they can throw them out. But they also want to be certain that their parents are still around and paying attention. The problem within the Rio family is that the eating disorder became the tie that binds. The illness served the purpose of engaging her distracted parents, and Tara undoubtedly had an unconscious fear that if she was not sick, her parents would revert to being distracted.

Linda's internal distraction was one disappointment that resulted in Tara feeling neglected. The more profound disappointment that Tara experienced was Linda's inability to protect herself and the children from Lou's abuse. I believe this was one of the most important factors in Tara's development of an eating disorder and other self-destructive behaviors. In order to better understand the variety of ways this issue affect girls, it is important to understand how development would normally proceed for teenage girls.

### The Role of Fathers

Adolescence is the time when kids are supposed to spread their wings and experiment with flying on their own. There is a drive to spend more time away from home, practice leaning on peers more, and explore new thinking. Breaking away from mothers is usually more difficult than breaking away from fathers because moms are more symbolic of a nurturing, safe environment. Yet fathers play a crucial role at this developmental stage. Stronger identifications with fathers allow both sons and daughters to break away from the maternal attachment. If fathers are not present, either physically or emotionally, or are perceived as dangerous, this differentiation becomes more challenging.

Sons have an easier time of differentiating from mothers because they are a different gender. There is a built-in identification with men. Obviously, differentiating for daughters is more difficult because they are the same gender. Consequently, finding common ground to accomplish a strong identification with their fathers is crucial. If fathers drop this ball, then the daughters will often unconsciously look for boyfriends or other things, like an eating disorder, to fill the gap. Interestingly, and unfortunately, one of the first ways that Tara and Lou try to find common ground during adolescence was through dieting. They join forces in an effort at self-improvement through trying to lose weight.

Tara's relationship with her dad seems to have presented a number of difficulties for her. First, his occasional critical view of her may have confirmed and enflamed her simmering low self-esteem. She comes to believe that the most important man in her life sees her as inadequate and deserving of punishment. This belief eventually manifests itself in a variety of self-destructive behaviors, including cutting herself. The distance between them also made it more difficult for Tara to identify with him to help with the differentiation from her mother. Finally, his poor treatment of Linda—and her tolerance of it—may have led Tara to believe that women do not deserve to be respected, and accordingly, she actually begins to treat her mother in an increasingly disrespectful way. She is in essence accomplishing the identification with her father, but not in a self-enhancing way.

It is extremely important to note how powerful and important their fathers' opinions and comments can be to daughters at this age. One "cutting" remark from a father to a psychologically vulnerable teenaged daughter can trigger the type of self-destructive thoughts and feelings that Tara describes. Unfortunately, it can even wipe out nine previous positive comments from the father. It has been my clinical experience that fathers consistently underestimate their importance with their teenage daughters. This is a great tragedy. Their daughters need them more during these years than ever before, even if they don't act like it. How they treat their wives is also extremely important. Daughters closely watch how their fathers treat their mothers and form beliefs about the value of women and the rules of conduct between men and women who are supposed to love and respect each other.

Tara's eating disorders served several purposes for her regarding her family. She eats in response to being alone after school and at night. Thousands of latchkey kids binge eat when they are alone in the afternoon after school. Food is one of the most powerful symbols of love and connection. Overeating in response to loneliness is normative. Tara's purging also has symbolic meaning. In addition to protecting herself against unwanted calories, she is ragefully rejecting the substitute for her mother and father. She is acting out the love-hate relationship she is going through with both parents. She is symbolically taking them in and throwing them out. Tara's deterioration also forces the family to pay attention to her and to the problems in the family. Her illness will force the abuse issues into the open and provoke change.

## Cultural Norms and Values

Family dynamics are strongly influenced by the culture of the time. Therefore, Linda and Lou's actions need to be understood within this context. Linda is caught dead center in the confusing time of early feminism in California. She got married in the late 1960s, which was the beginning of a time that questioned what women's roles should be. Linda's diary entries vividly capture the confusion and ambivalence about the value of motherhood versus a career that many young women struggled with during this time. Linda's paralysis regarding Lou's abuse was also, unfortunately, normative. Verbal, physical, and sexual abuse was hardly talked about in this era, and there were few resources available to deal with it when it was discussed. Frighteningly, standard treatment texts in the field of eating disorders published in the early to mid 1980s made little mention of the role of abuse in understanding and treating eating disorders. This was truly a "large elephant in the living room" that few people were talking about.

Lou was also caught in this cultural cross fire. When the abuse issue was finally talked about openly, Lou admitted that his rage toward the people he loves the most was inexcusable. These were, however, confusing and frustrating times for a man raised in a traditional Italian family. Going into psychotherapy to get help with the challenges of marriage and family or a mood disorder was not much of an option for men from Lou's background in the 1960s, 1970s, and 1980s. So he was left to his own devices to figure out how to become a man, husband, and father 3,000 miles away from his roots and in a hotbed of liberalism and feminism.

## WHAT SHOULD I DO IF I SUSPECT MY CHILD HAS AN EATING DISORDER?

Despite what we as parents might wish, it is unlikely that a child will just "grow out of" an eating disorder. And just as you wouldn't expect a child's broken leg to heal on its own, you cannot expect a child to recover from an eating disorder on her own. An eating disorder is a sign that something is wrong within your child's life. Your child will need your love and support, and you will need to assemble the proper resources to get him or her on the path to healing.

The good news is, even though our understanding of how these illnesses begin and how to treat them is only about 30 years old, we have made significant strides in our ability to help patients recover from eating disorders. As the parent, you will play one of the most important roles in your child's healing.

### GET HELP IMMEDIATELY

If you suspect your child has an eating disorder, get help *as soon as possible*. Early detection and intervention dramatically improve the chances of recovery. The first and most obvious warning sign is talk of going on a diet or wanting to lose weight. I urge you to take your child's wish to go on a diet as seriously as if she were requesting to have cosmetic surgery or take athletic performance enhancers like creatine or steroids. I'm sure you would thoroughly investigate what was on your child's mind and the potential medical side effects of those treatments. As mentioned earlier, it is very important to remember that exercising excessively or restricting calories, proteins, carbohydrates, or fats alters neurochemistry. For most people, this alteration will be innocent; for some, it will not. Take any interest your child has in dieting very seriously.

The following is a list of things that can signal that dieting or the drive for thinness is becoming a psychiatric illness:

- The weight loss continues beyond the original goal

- Defensiveness and unwillingness to talk about the continued weight loss

- Protests that they are still overweight despite being thin

- Weighing themselves daily or more

- Preoccupation with one area of the body, such as the stomach, hips, or thighs

- Phobic-like avoidance of certain food groups, such as fats or carbohydrates

- Increasing withdrawal from friends, family, and normal activities, accompanied by increased focus on exercise and weight control activities

- Increasingly ritualized food behavior such as cutting food into small bites, eating very slowly, and chewing excessively

- Increasing compulsiveness about exercise and an observable inability to sit still, such as constant leg rocking while sitting to burn calories

- Continuing to exercise through illness, injury, or adverse conditions like very inclement weather

- Increased secretiveness, which could signal the development of binge eating and purging

- Quickly leaving the table after meals to purge

- An overall deterioration in mood and activities as weight control behaviors increase

- Increasingly frantic denial that anything is wrong

Tara progressively developed most of these warning signs. Thankfully, she fought through her shame to let her mother know that she was drowning with depression and the eating disorder, and Linda was wise enough to take her seriously. Unfortunately, Lou made the mistake that many parents, particularly fathers, make when they learn of their daughters' symptoms. They minimize the potential danger. They treat the illness as a "fad diet gone bad" and believe that the child will "grow out of it." Unfortunately, the longer parents wait, the greater the likelihood that irreversible medical problems will occur and that the behaviors will become entrenched. The Rio family was also fortunate that Linda was a professional in the field and knew the importance of gathering a multidisciplinary team to help Tara.

## ASSEMBLE A MULTIDISCIPLINARY TREATMENT TEAM

Treating eating disorders requires an unusual integration of several types of health care professionals. A good team usually consists of a pediatrician or internist, a dietician, a psychotherapist, and a psychiatrist. In the following paragraphs, I'll highlight the role of each.

### Medical Evaluation

An initial physical by a physician is extremely important to rule out other medical conditions that could cause weight loss. The doctor will also need to make sure that your child is not in serious medical jeopardy. Prolonged malnutrition, low body weight, and purging behaviors can result in serious heart, kidney, brain, and bone problems. Tara had most of the more common medical symptoms associated with anorexia and bulimia.

Heart problems are usually the most immediate danger, and this was true for Tara. How does an eating disorder affect the heart? The body has to maintain a temperature of about 98 degrees to survive. Calories are the fuel that we burn to generate heat. If our energy expenditure exceeds our calorie intake, then our bodies start to burn fat to make up the difference. If the body exhausts its fat reserves, it will start burning lean muscle in order to stay warm. And as a muscle, the heart is one of the first organs that begins to be burned. This progressive burning makes the heart weaker and less effective. Low blood pressure develops and causes dizziness, fainting, and fatigue. Frighteningly, it is unclear whether the heart ever returns to its normal size and condition after a period of starvation.

Purging can also cause severe medical side effects. Self-induced vomiting and laxative abuse can severely dehydrate the body and destabilize electrolytes. Electrolytes are responsible for maintaining proper electrical conductivity in our bodies. If these electrolytes become abnormal, the heart becomes arrhythmic and the brain becomes vulnerable to seizures.

Another side effect of anorexia is osteoporosis, which is a bone disorder. Bone mass development and maintenance is dependent upon normal hormone production in women. When girls stop menstruating, a common symptom of anorexia, their bones don't continue to grow at a normal rate. This results in them having weak bones. Unfortunately, there is currently no way to offset this problem, so they will go through life with an abnormal vulnerability to bone fractures.

Finally, repeated vomiting causes stomach acid to rinse over the teeth, resulting in the erosion of dental enamel and increased tooth decay. Sadly, it appears that once dental enamel is lost, it can't be restored.

To tell the truth, we actually don't know what all of the long-term consequences of anorexia and bulimia will be. The larger number of young women who developed this illness as teenagers in the 1980s and 1990s are just now entering midlife. Historically, we have never had the opportunity to observe the long-term medical problems among a large number of women who had eating disorders as adolescents.

After your child's medical condition has been assessed, the next step is to begin nutritional rehabilitation. It is important to remember that the most important medication we need to give eating disorder patients is food. This is also the medication that they are most scared of, so having a dietician on your treatment team who is knowledgeable about eating disorders is crucial.

### Nutritional Therapy

The role of the dietician is critical since recovery cannot start until your child's nutrition has been stabilized and she is no longer bingeing or purging. Otherwise, it is like trying to accomplish psychological change with an alcoholic who is still drunk. Nothing is going to change until your child's brain chemistry is normalized and she has stopped the harmful behaviors. She cannot think clearly or deeply when she is starving to death.

For Tara, this became a crucial stumbling block in her treatment. The rest of the therapy she was getting was doomed until she stopped her destructive eating habits.

Your child's dietician will help her develop a healthy eating plan and will explain how nutrients work in the body and what happens when the body is malnourished. If your child has lost a dangerous amount of weight, the dietician will help her gradually increase her calorie intake, slowly bringing her weight to a healthy level.

The dietician's ability to get your child to eat will be highly dependent upon the psychotherapist's ability to help her find other ways to cope with her difficulties rather than starving or bingeing and purging. So having an informed psychotherapist on the team is equally crucial.

### Psychotherapy

As I discussed earlier, there are many factors that can contribute to the development of an eating disorder. It is the psychotherapist's job to assess the psychological factors that are bothering your child and develop a treatment plan to relieve them. Most psychotherapists deliver care through individual, group, and family therapy. They use a variety of techniques, including cognitive-behavioral therapy, psychodynamic therapy, art therapy, movement therapy, body image therapy, relapse training, meditation, biofeedback, assertiveness training, and the 12-step model.

Cognitive-behavior therapy has been proven to be particularly effective with eating disorders. Consequently, this should be a standard inclusion in any treatment plan. Likewise, family therapy has proven to be highly effective and should be a routine part of the treatment plan.

I believe that family therapy contributed the most to Tara's recovery. It was during family therapy that her dad's verbal and physical abuse was finally acknowledged. Tara was also able to confront her mother regarding her disappointments with her. These were steps that, I believe, put them all on the road to healing.

## Medication Therapy

The role of the psychiatrist is to recommend medications that have been proven to be helpful with the related illnesses of depression, anxiety, obsessions, compulsions, and ADHD. Although there are virtually no medications designed just for eating disorders, the Selective Serotonin Reuptake Inhibitor (SSRI) medications such as Prozac have been particularly useful in the treatment of all of these disorders. In fact, the research is clear that the combination of these medications and psychotherapy produces the best outcomes.

This is the one area of Tara's care that I believe could have been improved. She clearly had a major depressive disorder yet was not placed on medication. I think the proper medication would have helped speed her recovery.

# CHOOSE THE RIGHT SETTING FOR RECOVERY

Once the treatment team has made their assessment, they will recommend where and how often treatment should occur. We always try to do the simplest and least disruptive thing first. For most families, this would be an outpatient intervention that would include weekly visits to the dietician and multiple visits to the psychotherapist for individual and family therapy. Group therapy may also be recommended. Visits to the pediatrician and psychiatrist may occur less often once medical stability has been achieved and medications have been started.

If progress becomes stalled using the model described above, the team will most likely recommend intensifying treatment through the use of a partial hospital program. Patients in these programs go to the hospital for several hours a day, but they continue to reside at home. Not all communities have this treatment option, however, so if outpatient care is failing, the next step is often inpatient treatment.

About one-third of the patients who begin outpatient care will need to eventually enter an inpatient program. This may be necessary for several reasons. The most common reason is that the outpatient intervention has not been enough to stop the problem behaviors. The patient needs the containment of the hospital to stop the starving, overexercising, bingeing, and purging. More rarely, a patient's weight may get so low that the treatment team needs the medical support of the hospital to carefully monitor the early stages of refeeding. Some patients die as a result of "refeeding syndrome." This occurs when weight is restored faster than the cardiovascular system can accommodate it.

I'm often asked why it's so hard to get patients with eating disorders, particularly those in inpatient programs, to eat or stop the bingeing and purging. The explanation goes back to our earlier discussion of anorexia being comparable to a severe phobia and bulimia to a severe addiction.

The treatment for phobia is a form of "systematic desensitization." This means that we progressively require the patient to move toward the feared object while helping her find new ways to cope with the anxiety associated with that object. The feared object for patients with eating disorders is weight gain, fat, or other feared food groups. The new coping mechanisms include the techniques mentioned in the psychotherapy section. If your child's eating disorder takes the form of a phobia, it is extremely important to note that her anxiety will get worse as she moves closer and closer to the feared thing. The treatment will actually worsen her anxiety in the short run.

To understand why this is so, let's use the case of someone with an elevator phobia as an example. This person's worst moment is when she is standing on the threshold of the elevator. This is the moment when she is going to have to take a "leap of faith." The moment she steps into the elevator, although she is very anxious, she instantly realizes that she is still alive, and so her anxiety crests and begins to abate. It is the threshold of the elevator that is the scariest, not actually being in the elevator. For patients with eating disorders, the equivalent of the elevator threshold is usually a symbolic weight, the return of their menstrual cycle, the fit of an anorexic pair of jeans, or some other way they have concretely measured their size and shape. Furthermore, if we do not take elevator-phobic patients all the way into the elevator, we know that their avoidant defenses will immediately return. Similarly, it is crucial that eating disorder patients be fully weight restored. If we stop short of their phobic threshold, then the likelihood of relapse after hospitalization doubles.

For people whose eating disorders are like an addiction, there is some physiological and psychological attraction to the binge eating, purging, or hyper-exercise. If this is the case for your child, you need to remember that she is compelled to do these behaviors. If she stops, she will manifest many of the characteristics of an addict in detox. She will likely do just about anything to get to the altered state associated with the behaviors.

This was the case with Tara. Writing about this time in her life, she states, "All I know for sure is that from the moment I hung my head over the toilet and felt the rush of adrenaline reach my temples, I knew I was in love. Like a heroine addict longing for his next hit, I would sit in class and daydream about when I would get the next opportunity to vomit. I craved the high it gave me, and I was obsessed with planning the ways I would elevate that high."

Once again, many of the techniques mentioned in the psychotherapy section are helpful with this group. Additionally, some of the 12-step techniques that have been successfully used in the treatment of addictions are useful with this group.

## HOW DO I KNOW IF MY CHILD IS ON THE ROAD TO RECOVERY?

Whatever unique combination of therapy your child's doctors prescribe, she will likely go through several phases in her recovery. Be aware that in the first phase, the responsibility for recovery falls mostly on the parents' shoulders. We saw this in Tara's case, as Linda and Lou got her into psychotherapy and nutrition counseling. Yet, despite their efforts, Tara continued to purge.

Gradually, however, Tara became more motivated within herself to end her relationship with her illness. Even with greater motivation, however, she struggled with the common problem of occasionally "falling off the wagon." This will likely happen to your child as well.

Be assured that relapses are a routine part of the course of the illness. I tell my patients and their families that recovery often unfolds as a process of taking two steps forward and one step back. Of course, this can be tough to deal with if you and your child tend to be perfectionistic and overachieving. Yet relapses can be beneficial in that they allow us to work on these larger personality vulnerabilities.

Perhaps the most important factor in recovery is what is called "the readiness factor." Even if you and your child's clinicians are providing optimal care, your child may simply not be ready to recover. It is extremely important to recognize that readiness to recover includes two components: willingness and ability. Willingness, of course, refers to motivation. Ability refers to several factors, including cognitive maturity, psychological maturity, and the extent of related illnesses such as depression and anxiety. Sustained recovery is usually not possible until both of these components are operating in tandem.

Once both of these components are in place, patients will often have an epiphany, an awakening or moment of truth. Something they read or something someone says results in a revelation that propels them into a fuller recovery. Recovered alcoholics use the phrase "getting it" to describe this latter stage of recovery.

Tara's epiphany came while watching *Oprah*. For her, hearing the words and confidence of a guest one day became a transforming moment, and her recovery solidified. While Tara may struggle with body image issues or thoughts of purging in the future, the illness will never occupy the same space in her mind that it did before that moment. Is she fully recovered? I have asked Tara this question. She humbly, with respect for how powerful this illness can be, answers . . . yes.

## RECOVERY RATES

When your child is in the midst of recovery, time may seem as if it's standing still as you watch her struggle and, occasionally, relapse. The good news is that approximately two-thirds of eating disorder patients will be cured or have significant improvement within 1 to 2 years through the use of medications and individual, group, and family therapy. For the other one-third, who often have to enter more intensive, residentially based treatment, the length of time to recovery is much longer—7 to 10 years. Still, upwards of 75 percent of these patients will fully recover. Combining the recovery rates from both outpatient and inpatient treatment, we find that roughly 80 to 90 percent of eating disorder patients will successfully overcome their illnesses. Unfortunately, approximately 10 percent will chronically struggle and eventually die from complications related to their illnesses.

I believe that Tara and her family are to be commended for courageously sharing their painful story. It is my hope that by reading about their brave struggles, you, too, have gained hope and insight that will lead both you and your child safely on the path to recovery. With greater education and awareness about eating disorders, I believe that we can improve the recovery rates even further and perhaps one day be able to save each and every child from the grip of these powerful diseases.

Dr. Johnson is founder and director of the eating disorders program at Laureate Psychiatric Clinic and Hospital in Tulsa. He is professor of clinical psychology at the University of Tulsa, associate professor of psychiatry at the University of Oklahoma College of Medicine, and president of the National Eating Disorders Association. He was the founding editor of the *International Journal of Eating Disorders* and a founding member of the Academy for Eating Disorders and the Eating Disorders Research Society. Dr. Johnson did his graduate work at Oklahoma State University and Yale University School of Medicine. He formerly held faculty appointments at the University of Chicago and Northwestern University medical schools. He has authored three books and more than 70 scientific articles and has been the recipient of several distinguished contribution awards.

## NEWSLETTERS AND BOOKS

*Eating Disorders Today: A Newsletter for Recovering Individuals and Their Loved Ones*
This newsletter, which is published by Gürze Books, provides self-help advice from respected experts in the field of eating disorders as well as information on what family members can do to provide support, how to get insurance coverage for treatment, and strategies for dealing with relapse. To subscribe, call (800) 756-7533 or see the Gürze Books contact information below.

**Gürze Books**
PO Box 2238
Carlsbad, CA 92018
(800) 756-7533
www.bulimia.com
Contact Gürze Books for a wide range of books on eating disorders for both professionals and consumers. Their Web site is well-organized and includes dozens of links to helpful organizations devoted to eating disorders.

## NATIONAL ORGANIZATIONS

**Academy for Eating Disorders**
6728 Old McLean Village Drive
McLean, VA 22101
(703) 556-9222
www.aedweb.org

This multidisciplinary professional organization focuses on Anorexia Nervosa, Bulimia Nervosa, Binge Eating Disorder, and related disorders. The Academy believes that effective treatment for eating disorder patients requires professionals from various disciplines working together. Visit their Web site to learn more about their work or to become an affiliate member.

**American Association for Marriage and Family Therapy (AAMFT)**
112 South Alfred Street
Alexandria, VA 22314-3061
(703) 838-9808
www.aamft.org
To find an AAMFT therapist in your area, visit
www.TherapistLocator.net.

**Dads and Daughters (DADs)**
34 East Superior Street, Suite 200
Duluth, MN 55802
(888) 824-3237
www.dadsanddaughters.org
Dads and Daughters is a national education and advocacy group for fathers and daughters. DADs provides tools to strengthen father-daughter relationships and transform pervasive cultural messages that value daughters more for how they look than who they are.

**Depression and Bipolar Support Alliance (DBSA)**
730 North Franklin Street, Suite 501
Chicago, IL 60610-7204
(800) 826-3632
www.dbsalliance.org
This organization's Web site contains detailed information on mood disorders and a database you can search to find a local support group.

**Eating Disorder Referral and Information Center**
2923 Sandy Pointe, Suite 6
Del Mar, CA 92014-2052
(858) 792-7463
www.edreferral.com
This organization provides free information and referrals to treatment centers and private practitioners for all forms of eating disorders.

**Eating Disorders Coalition for Research, Policy, and Action (EDC)**
611 Pennsylvania Avenue SE #423
Washington, DC 20003-4303
(202) 543-9570
www.eatingdisorderscoalition.org
The EDC works to influence federal policy on eating disorders.

**The International Association of Eating Disorders Professionals
Foundation (IAEDP)**
PO Box 1295
Pekin, IL 61555-1295
(309) 346-3341
www.iaedp.com
This foundation is dedicated to providing first-rate education and
training for eating disorders professionals. It also promotes public
awareness of eating disorders and assists in prevention efforts.
Visitors to their Web site can search a membership directory to find
a local therapist who specializes in eating disorders.

**National Association of Anorexia Nervosa and Associated
Disorders (ANAD)**
PO Box 7
Highland Park, IL 60035
(847) 831-3438
www.anad.org
Visit this association's Web site to find a local support group, read
extensive information on eating disorders, including a self-
evaluation checklist, or access an interactive bulletin board where
you can read letters from others who are living with or recovering
from an eating disorder.

**National Eating Disorders Association**
603 Stewart Street, Suite 803
Seattle, WA 98101
(206) 382-3587
Information and referral helpline: (800) 931-2237
www.nationaleatingdisorders.org
The National Eating Disorders Association is dedicated to the
elimination of eating disorders and body dissatisfaction. Visit their
Web site for information on eating disorders or call their national
helpline for support or a referral to a local physician, nutritionist,
or counselor who specializes in eating disorders.

# ACKNOWLEDGMENTS

First and foremost, we'd like to thank Lou and Gregg for being selfless enough to allow us to share our family's story. You, along with Jackie Rio, spent many hours of tearful family discussions about the emotional impact this project may have on our family. You joined us on this journey to relive past, sometimes painful, experiences and complete the final chapter on our family's healing.

Together we also thank other members of our family who know all too well the struggles we've experienced. You are deeply loved and respected for your own lives and for your understanding of ours.

There are many others who have touched our lives, some mentioned in these diary accounts. Your names have been changed to protect your privacy, but you will always be remembered for touching us in special and unique ways.

We are enormously appreciative of the expertise of Lou Cinquino at Rodale, who fought tirelessly for this project and treated us, and the deeply personal nature of this story, with the utmost respect. Additionally, we thank our agent, Jodie Rhodes, who believed in the value of our story and worked tirelessly to bring this project to the attention of the publishing world.

We are honored and grateful for the opportunity to collaborate with Dr. Craig Johnson. In addition to his renowned expertise, he brought a unique sensitivity to our project. Thank you, Craig, for your valuable insight into the depths of our pain and healing.

Most of all, we hope the three young girls in our lives benefit from our struggles and triumphs and learn to value the mother-daughter bond, no matter how strained it may become at times.

*Additional acknowledgments from Tara:*

I'd like to thank Mitch for playing the role of leading man in this story and continuing to play the role of leading man in our daughters' lives. Thank you for allowing me to share intimate details of our relationship in the hope that it might help others.

I want to thank Melissa for being the friend I trusted as my "other set of eyes." Thank you to Amber for your unwavering support and encouragement and for always being my "milk" when I needed it. And to Kim, thank you for standing by me through my illness and continuing to pull me from the depths of my depression more times than I care to recall.

And to my mother, thank you for having the strength to confront painful memories and the courage to have your life displayed and scrutinized. I don't know any other mother who would have agreed to expose herself, as much as you did, for the sole purpose of helping her daughter, and others, heal.

*Additional acknowledgments from Linda:*

Thank you to my colleagues and associates at New Beginnings Counseling Center who encouraged and listened to ideas and feelings about this book and many of whom lived through the times these pages tell. Words fall short of expressing the depth of my gratitude to Tom Archbald, Susan Baker, Bill Gibson, Miriam Hamideh, Susan Hardy, Dree Miller, Raphael Serrano, and Barbara St. Amand, with a special thanks to Susan Richter for your early editorial input and immense eating disorders expertise. I would also like to thank Monte Elchoness for providing writing mentorship, Barbara Morris for self-esteem bolstering, and my many other professional colleagues and friends who have been supportive through my experience of living, and writing, this story.

I am eternally grateful to all the mothers, fathers, grandparents, and caregivers who have honored me with their presence in my psychotherapy practice through the years. Most important, thank you to the children and teens who have come to my office and taught me the essentials about life. It was your courage that inspired me to trust that the telling of this very personal story of my own family would be the right thing to do.

My mother, Rita Slason, bravely and without hesitation gave us total freedom to write anything pertaining to her part in our lives. Unfortunately, space did not permit a more thorough multigenerational examination into aspects of our family history, which contributed positively and negatively to our difficulties and triumphs. My undying thanks to you, Mom, for your never-ending belief in me, especially when I definitely did not believe in myself.

I must honor and thank my coauthor and daughter, Tara. This book was your golden and brave idea. You wrote first the words of a troubled and lonely young girl, later a blossomed young woman desiring to help others who have not yet found their voice. Tara, you wanted to write this book for over a decade. When the time was right, you tirelessly researched publishers and agents and did the hard work necessary to get this story told. Despite everything we have been through, I am honored beyond belief that you wanted my input and whatever I had to offer to this project. We've been through a lot, kiddo. I love you more than words can ever say.

The passion for this project came from the hope that we, as mother and daughter, had indeed learned something from our experiences that would help others struggling with similar issues. When the anxiety of sharing such intimate details of our lives became overwhelming, it was this hope that saw us through.

We hope readers will find comfort in knowing that other families experience similar struggles, support is available, and recovery is attainable.

*Acknowledgments from Craig Johnson, Ph.D.:*

I would like to thank Tara and Linda for the invitation to participate in this unique project. This is a very, very brave thing that they have done. I have enormous respect for their willingness to deal directly and openly with difficult issues. I would also like to thank Lou Rio for his willingness to acknowledge the mistakes he made within his family. I believe that his openness in this regard will help prevent other men from making similar mistakes.

I would also like to thank the staff and administration of Laureate Psychiatric Clinic and Hospital for giving me the time to work on this project. In order for me to do this, others had to cover for part of my clinical and administrative responsibilities. I work with a very capable staff, which has been one of the great pleasures of my career.

Lou Cinquino and the staff at Rodale made this project easy. Those magicians made my fairly boring academic writing readable.

Finally, I would like to thank my wife, Patti, and my glorious teenage children, Laura and Ben. I have asked Laura to review many books about eating disorders that have been written for children and teens. Over the last several years she has read them, handed them back, and said "same old, same old." She declared this book "interesting," which is a large part of the reason I agreed to participate. Likewise, Patti has been a great sounding board, editor, and overall partner in many of these projects. Thanks to Ben for being involved with baseball, racing midget cars, and a thousand other things that have nothing to do with the field of eating disorders.

# INDEX

Jan 5, 88

D-

I'm trying out for the swim team! I can't believe I'm doing this. I had to go & pick the 1 sport that you have to wear a bathing suit in. If I didn't love swimming so much I would never do this. But I always wear 2 or 3 suits so you can't see my body as much. I also take my towel right to the edge of the pool & drop it right before I dive into the water. Most of the girls on the team do this. We're all sooooo self consious of our bodies. Every day in the locker room you can hear almost every girl complain about her body. At least we all have that in common. I HAVE TO STOP EATING! Dressing out everyday